IMPROV & HOPE

From the Journal Writings of
Alec Williams

Wendy D. Fambro

ISBN 978-1-300-42525-0

Preface

I never met Alec Williams. I know nothing more about him than any of you would know upon encountering the few pages of journaling, poetry, and music he left behind after his brief sojourn on this earth. But I had the joy of knowing his mother, Andria, for the last two years of her life, and agreed to write this book just two weeks before she died. It was a mother's dying wish, and one I had the capacity to fulfill. Or, so I thought.

The request was a simple one: read through the journals that Alec had kept and edit them into some kind of readable form, and then donate the final project, along with the source materials, to a college or university where they would be archived for future use. What use? That was never clear. But Andria believed there was value to her son's thoughts and works, and that they should be preserved.

Again, the request was straightforward. Despite the fact that the journals proved to be dense, complex, and fragmented - meant for Alec's own use, not for an evening's read before bedtime - it was not necessarily my job to make them clear, simply to organize them for preservation. My problem was that while Andria wished to share these works out of love for her son, I wanted to honor her son out of love for Andria. And love can sometimes take a simple task and make it complicated.

During this year of writing (or, more often - NOT writing), I have struggled with the question of why anyone would, or should, care about this book? Let's take YOU, for example. You never met Alec. You never knew Andria. There are nearly 7 billion people on this earth at this moment who might benefit from your attention, but Alec is not one of them. He never did anything in his lifetime that went very far beyond his own front door - in fact, very little of it even went beyond his own mind. In many ways, Alec lived an exceptionally tiny life, and in a very real way, his tiny life mattered to only one other person - his mother - who has also departed this world. So, who is left to care?

My family will tell you that not long ago, I walked away from a job, a solid paycheck, and benefits - including the house that came with the job - because after 2 years, it had become clear that it was a meaningless pursuit. So, while I signed a written agreement with Andria to create this book shortly before she died, the contract alone would not have kept me on the project. Not even the sense of obligation to Andria would hold me in front of the keyboard (though the "promise" holds more power than the paycheck.) It is, rather, the sense that somehow, there is a cosmic consequence in affirming that there once was a boy named Alec Williams who lived, breathed, took up space, struggled, thought, learned, became, created, existed, and loved, and then moved on. There is something in all of us that needs to know that our lives have mattered - that the breaths we take shape the world, even if that shape is forever unclear.

I learned early on that the greatest compliment one could receive from Andria was that one was "interesting." She had a lively mind, and it mattered to her that those around her were intellectually stimulating. She enjoyed words, phrases, ideas. And she thoroughly enjoyed Alec for his varied interests and his ability to weave new thoughts from his studies. I was genuinely flattered to know that she also found me to be "interesting," and was grateful that even as her body failed, her mind remained clear until the end. Just days before her passing, we discussed her time spent living in Sumatra, Jazz, current events, and the Ghanaian soccer team. She showed me her latest jewelry acquisitions - large rings that one of her most cherished friends had chosen for her. She confessed that she believed she had become a better person in these last few years of living alone, because she no longer felt the sense of inadequacy she had known, first as a daughter, then as a wife, and finally a mother. She said this without any sense of judgment against her younger self, just as a point of "fact." And, finally, she said that her only regret in dying was that she would be leaving behind such interesting people for whom she had come to care.

In the year since she died, I have missed my interesting friend, and after spending these past months moving between her autobiographical memories, and Alec's journals, I wish I could have just one moment back with her to say - you were not a perfect mother, but you were the perfect mother for your son. Well done.

Introduction

The most difficult part of this writing task, it turns out, was deciding how best to structure the material. I will not torture you with the many ideas that were tried and rejected. I will simply share with you a key to understanding the final format. This is a book written in three voices: Andria's, Alec's, and my own. My assignment was to edit and present Alec's thoughts as recorded in his journals. After spending months wading through these pages, it became increasingly clear that his words would be more authentic if they were set within the context of his life, and the only person who could offer a view into that world was his mother, Andria. But, even with both voices available to me (in a limited fashion), I knew that the very nature of my task in sorting, editing, and juxtaposing these two perspectives would impact the final manuscript. I also knew that I was not an objective, disengaged freelancer hired for some clearly defined project. I was a friend who could not help but approach these journals with a bias toward finding value in them. For that reason, I finally decided that it was most appropriate to just join the conversation.

In the pages that follow, then, you will begin from hearing the story of Andria and Alec's life together as remembered by Andria. These remembrances were gleaned from tape recordings made over time, by interviews conducted, and by conversations shared. They are almost entirely in Andria's own words, though, knowing how strongly she valued proper grammar, phrasing, and vocabulary, I made minor adjustments to best reflect her language. (Note: passages in Andria's voice are reproduced here in

Homemade Apple font – a somewhat more legible

version of her own handwriting.)

The reflections from Andria are followed by pieces from Alec's journals, along with samples of his poetry. Here is where most of the editing work was done - simply in choosing which journal notes to share under which part of the life story being told. It is completely subjective as Alec clearly was not writing with these "chapters" in his mind. Likewise, to better serve the narrative flow, I made decisions regarding which journal entries to include within the book, and what to leave out. I have no doubt that Alec would disagree, and vehemently, with many of my decisions. While I did make choices about which pieces to share and where, I did not edit his words. I say this partly to assure you that Alec's words are Alec's words, and also to *warn* you that these are Alec's words - unedited. They are harsh, sometimes foul, often mind-boggling, and always Alec. As he himself stated: "I don't edit my reality." (20b) (Note: passages in Alec's voice are reproduced here in *Mareen's Print* font – again, a reasonable facsimile of his actual handwriting.)

And, though I did, in fact, rearrange the order of appearance of these journal entries, they are not, as you might think, disconnected *because* of that process. Within the journals themselves, Alec's pen jumps from thought to thought, from topic to topic, from a philosophical outpouring, to a note about his next move in *Dungeons and Dragons*, to a song lyric he is working on, to a rant about his sister, to a comment on a movie, to a reminder about medications - all on one page. But in Alec's words:

"People who criticize me for failure to be comprehensible are those bitching about a cut stone because they will look at one, perhaps two facets at most, and ignore the whole." (18b)

The full text of his journals are available via www.AlecWilliams.com, and the numbers noted in parentheses following each entry in this book can be matched to the original journals if desired.

Finally, I offer a brief reflection following the words of mother and son. It was necessary for me to write these for my own journey through this project, but it is not necessary for you to read them unless you so desire. (Note: my reflections are recorded here in Arial font.)

For Andria...

Andria

On January 8, 1969, Alec Jenkyn Williams arrived in a blinding rage. The doctor induced labor before the cervix had softened, so for 8 hours, the baby's head had been used as a battering ram, which we can imagine he didn't like one bit.

The next time I saw him, Alec was in the recovery room where he had been laid in a plastic bassinette. I was rather surprised to see that his eyes appeared to be roaming around the room, studying his surroundings. I hadn't expected him to be cognizant to his whereabouts to that degree, or interested in them, but my impression was that he was curiously aware.

Alec was a rather difficult child to look after. As an infant, and later as a toddler, he never did form a pattern of sleep until he was close to 4 years old, and since somebody had to look after him, my nights were very interrupted. On the positive side, we spent a lot of time together. Alec liked to be carried around - he liked body contact, and he liked a change of scene. So, I could put him in a playpen with 20 toys and within just a few minutes, he'd be yearning to get out.

As a little one, there were just a few signs of the excessive nervous response that would shape his life (and mine.) I remember taking him in for his six weeks' check-up, and when the doctor clapped his hands to check Alec's startle reflex, his whole body jumped a full inch off the table. The doctor, looking impressed, remarked, "Great startle reflex." Well, with the view of hindsight, it was far too great a reaction, but nobody knew to look at it in that fashion at that time.

I remember, too, that even in those early months, we couldn't play a record that had sudden loud sounds in it compared to soft sounds. The shift in volume would cause Alec discomfort and he would let his displeasure be known. These kinds of reactions didn't seem to add up to anything at the time, nor was I looking to add them up.

Alec

I know I'll die before I get old. (8a)

By trying to deny my inherent other-than-else, I just made myself worse. Born internal and enlightened, they will out - by fits, etc., if needed. (9b)

The price of consciousness is self-consciousness (10b)

Beyond "I AM" is "I AM WHAT?" (11b)

A DNA chain of spiraling paradox, that's me. (14b)

What was your face like before you were born? Two opposing mirrors. (18b)

I am the last awakening of the Old Ways. (21b)

Born in winters. I am Ragnarok. (24b)

If anyone's to blame, it's me, for being born. A minimal few wanted it. The opposition was far stronger (the universe?) Jerry wanted me dead; sis wanted me dead (or at least) in the head, so give me the blame. I'll take the power and curse you All. (15d)

I was conceived in a lie and born to break them. (35d)

We are brought into being moment by moment by the thoughts of that which never was. (18d)

KNOWING (#13)

To know
What is going on
I'd like it
I think sometimes...
But then
I think again
All this...
Thinking
What's it for?

Everything
To know everything
I could relax
To know
Why
Or even
How
I think sometimes...

Why

I think sometimes...

Nothing

To know what is going on

I'd like it

I think sometimes...

Nothing

(20b)
Snowfalls
These winter blossoms
Could one of them be me?

Reflection

Mother and son, looking back, visiting that far ago place of the beginning, and neither of them pretending that it was a time of innocence.

As a mother myself, I hear in Andria's memories the weariness mixed with pride, the painful knowledge of what was to come, stirred with the preserved wonder of new life. She may not have yet recognized the signs of his physical challenges that would impact his mind and spirit, but she understood that, in many ways, this baby would mold her more than she would ever shape him. And she marveled at him - a force of nature swaddled by nurses and given into her care.

Alec. Living in a constant state of heightened physicality and awareness. Throughout his journals, Alec examines his lifetime, looking back into the time before he was born and ahead into the time beyond his death. More than anything, his passionate claim on his own life, and his insistence on revealing his own meaning, ensured that I would know him - not just as words scribbled in spiral notebooks, but also as a lung-breathing, heart-beating soul. A window is opened to a young man who grates against the knowledge? belief? that he is unwanted by those closest to him on the human plane, while exploring alternative sources of value and connectedness.

There is such power in the containment of language that Alec uses. There is no way to know how much time passes between each thought. I find myself reading through a page as I would read any other work, only to return to the top to try again - this time, pausing to breathe between each entry, to let each thought stand on its own. Like his mother, I marvel at the complexity of ponderings that pass through Alec's mind onto the page, his self-awareness - at times painful and untethered, at other times pulsating with calm certitude about his place and purpose in the world. And then, the sweetness of poetry that interrupts the mental gymnastics to let one just drift for a few moments.

Throughout his journals, I am most inspired by his ability to infuse his words with occasional and subtle humor, reminding himself (and me) that his world contained not only the struggle to live with and beyond his physical/mental challenges, but also laughter and, yes, love.

Andria

We had a little problem on our hands in that sleep, for Alec, was not a very necessary article. Two hours at a time would do just fine. He'd wake us then and Alec would be offered a bottle, which he'd gladly take, but with no intention of going back to sleep. Inevitably, he wanted to come downstairs from his room, and to be held and carried about. Alec always preferred movement and changes in scenery, so nights were sort of perambulatory ones for a long time in the Jenkyn-Williams household.

The same was true during the daytime. Having been put in the playpen with a half a dozen or more things to do, Alec would ignore them all and within minutes he would be howling to get out and for the world to improve. Much of my time was spent trying to get things done around the house with a baby attached to my shoulder.

As Alec got older, I would put him in a stroller for long, long walks - both morning and afternoon. Alec was quite content so long as the scenery was changing. He particularly liked supermarkets and other crowded places. People gave him a lot of attention and would often remark about what an alert and interested baby he was. A friend of mine, who had three sons, said that this was only because he was a baby, and that everyone noticed babies. But, one day, after she had watched Alec for me for a short time, she handed him back and said, "You win. They do look at him a lot."

Alec

Not "I think therefore I am," but "I ask therefore things act." (1b)

Someone may communicate a wisdom they are incapable of expressing. (12b)

Children have a natural affinity for magic. I have been unknowingly using magic since childhood to make up for deficiencies - without getting Freud about shiz, for me, this is return to childhood - Natural Existence (see UG Krisnamurti) PLUS. (14c)

The stimming reveals the truth of untruth
the associations between enigmas,
the unmeaning meaning,
the simultaneity of alpha/omega,
infinite depth and shallowness,
the land beyond duality,
a land of uncountable living
options waiting to flesh
the true nature of chaos,
all succeeding each other at speeds unmeasurable.
There must be space to move at speed,
there must be freedom or there is no life. (3d)

Reflection

What mother doesn't think that their own child is beautiful, exceptional, a step forward on the evolutionary scale? My first daughter was happy, personable, and adorable - she was an "easy" baby. My second was equally adorable, but less content with her own infancy, and, like Alec, was not particularly enamored with sleep. Those late night roamings bonded us, though, in a way that was distinct in that I know I felt more protective of her. This early connection between Alec and Andria, forged through endless hours of roaming a quiet house and a darkened neighborhood, in some ways foreshadowed their life together - apart, unseen, protected.

Alec, who might have easily felt disempowered by the circumstances of his life, wrote often of his will. He saw himself as impacting the world - as having a role to play, and focusing his energies toward that purpose. And the reality is that from the day he was born, the world shifted to accommodate his presence. Some of those around him resisted that disruption, while few - possibly his mother alone - embraced it.

"I ask, therefore things act." I have often returned to this line in Alec's journal. Do I too often wait for life to happen around me? Am I shy about asking? Do I let circumstances define my choices? Some who read these journals might see a young man suffering from schizophrenic-induced delusions of grandeur as he claims for himself an almost mythological role in the reordering of the cosmos. But, perhaps more of us suffer from delusions of insignificance - unaware of our own ability to cause the universe to act in response to our asking.

Andria

When Alec reached an age where he could sit up
and crawl about, he became interested in books.
We made sure that he had his own books from an
early age. We would sit on the couch for
extended periods of time naming shapes, object
and colors in his various picture books. Early
on he discovered that books were things of value
and that he was not allowed to take things off
the bookshelf. So whenever he wanted attention,
he would do just that - crawl over to the shelf,
and begin pulling the books down. Without fail,
somebody would rush over and put them back
saying, "No." Alec would then be pleased as can
be. As a family, we decided to not pay any
attention the next time he did it. A very puzzled
little boy sat among the pile of books looking as
if he didn't know what the trouble was. He
apparently digested this change in cause and

effect, and crawled off somewhere else, never going after a book again - except, of course, to read.

Alec learned to walk at the usual time, but was less inclined to talk. His father, a professor of linguistics, found this maddening. Whenever he took his turn changing Alec's diaper, he would say, "Cats meow, dogs bark, people talk - talk dammit!" To encourage language development, his father would also sing to him during these moments together. I, myself, talked to Alec all the time - but never using baby talk. There never was any of that in our house.

Even so, for those first two years, Alec never uttered a Dada or a Mama - he only made noises of distress. Then, suddenly, he began to say, "Please give me a glass of water" and "Thank you," stringing words together in meaningful phrases with a totally adult intonation pattern. You might have been speaking to a twenty year old.

His vocabulary grew rapidly due to being read to everyday. During the winter months, I must have gone through at least 15 books a day with him. Alec's ability to use language and to be able to communicate with it was very rough for him when playing with other children his age. One time, a little girl was visiting with her mother. She was only a couple of months younger than Alec. The mother and I watched as the children sat together on the floor, playing. Alec said, as clear as day, "Please pass the blocks, Candice." He repeated himself a few time, but got no response from little Candice. At that point Alec reached out and clubbed the poor child out of frustration.

Around that same time, we were having the house painted by a man who had been a teacher and who had discovered that he could do better as a house painter. Alec was in the habit of watching one of the children's shows on television, which was followed by a science show for older children (6th graders) The house painter came through one day and saw Alec watching this particular program. He looked at him curiously, went upstairs, came back and stopped to watch him again. After doing this several times, the painter followed me into the kitchen and said, "He is watching that program!" Adults found it fascinating that there was this small child surely tucking away information in that capacious head of his.

Alec

The answer is insufficient; the question is required, before and after every question. (3b)

My system is no system, nor is it theory; it is the phenomonation of question. (10b)

I know on a fundamental level (though due to Heisenberg, I DON'T know on said level) that I DON'T KNOW (again Heisenberg, so I don't KNOW I don't (then again perhaps H. blew it. I don't know THAT either, but with this much paradox I give myself leave to figure probabilistically H. was right)) one finds oneself in the position of proving oneself right by proving oneself wrong, just to jump sides long enough to reverse the polarity of the argument and continue modulating paradox. This is tiring. Believe me. (12d)

Imagination my forges fire
Intellect the icy stream
Reality my hammer and my anvil
Events are the product of my smithy. (31d)

Reflection

Alec was born into a home where the intellect was highly valued and nurtured. His father taught anthropological linguistics and Andria had a degree in languages and dabbled in writing. When I first met Andria, it was through an ad she had placed on Craigslist, looking for someone who would read to her. She was legally blind, and though she had an impressive library of books on tape, she was particularly interested in having someone read some of her own self-penned manuscripts back to her. I think we were equally delighted to find each other because I enjoyed her writings, and she appreciated my enjoyment of them. The manuscripts were from novel concepts put to paper years before, and she would sometimes pause to edit as we went along.

Her husband, it seems, had never approved of her pieces - or, had never taken them seriously. So, she would write in spurts, and rarely showed the stories to anyone. One fantasy piece that I much enjoyed reading aloud, she remembered having written in a fit of disgust. She and Alec had been spending a part of their summer vacation on a beach somewhere, and she had stocked up books for their time away. After reading aloud a story about dragons, she declared it to be a piece of tripe that she could have written in her sleep. She was so irritated by this lackluster piece of fantasy posing as real literature, that she spent the next few days scratching out a charming tale - using the same dragon motif - and put it in a box to be read, and appreciated, many years later by her new reader friend. She laughed and clapped her hands when the last words were read, and we put the pages back in the box for another day.

Alec's facility with language came naturally. His journals are rich in vocabulary, and in unique phrasings, in prose and poetry, images and evolved terminology. Before

Andria had come to me with her request to publish Alec's journals in an edited and accessible format, she had asked a few others. More than once she was told that the journals contained nothing more than the meaningless gibberish of a disturbed mind. Certainly some of it is disturb-*ing*, and some of its meanings are beyond my ability to interpret. But gibberish? This conclusion says more about the person reading the journals than the one who wrote them. On the other hand, would I have made the effort required to read Alec's words for meaning if I had not cared about his mother? Probably not. And that also says more about me than about the young man who sat in his room writing these pages, never giving a thought to me.

Andria

Thinking that I might "over-Mama" him, as mothers of children late in life often do I think, and because I thought he needed the society of his peers, I took him to visit a nursery school that had good reports when he was about two years and four months. The teachers were greatly amused by his ability to use the language and he seemed very much at home. But, at the time of our visit, it was after hours and the school was empty. The enrollment date had already passed, but the woman who ran the school, who had been trained in England in child education, said that, "You shouldn't wait until next year, he's ready now."

So, when Alec was still just two and two thirds years old, he began nursery school. We immediately discovered that while Alec had liked the empty schoolrooms just fine, the schoolrooms filled with children were another matter entirely. I would have to stay every morning in one of the rooms where books were kept and I would begin to read to him and would gradually gather a group of children, and then eventually he would slide off my lap and go exploring, and after an hour or sometimes a little more, he would come back to me and say, "It's alright, you can go now."

And so I would go. The teachers made no objection to this arrangement as small children regard any adult as a useful thing to have about - someone to help read stories and tie shoes, wipe noses and find mittens.

Alec remained in that school for three years. Despite the fact that he could have gone to kindergarten after the first two, the man who had become the head of the program said it would be better to keep him there for a third year because while thus far, Alec had been one of the smallest children in the school, now he would be one of the biggest. The director thought that this would do him good, which I thought was insightful, and likely true.

Within the classroom, Alec often moved from task to task rapidly. At one point, his teacher put him in at a table to do a painting and insisted he could not leave his chair until he finished. He was then probably about 3 and a half years old. Alec remembered this incident his whole life, interpreting it as having been injured and put upon by someone using authority over him - something he did <u>not</u> like at all. Looking back, I should have realized then that my son was not born to be a conformist. And he never was. I must say, I'm still glad of it.

Alec's interpretation of events could be quite astonishing and sometimes a little frightening. One incident stands out in my mind. I had been present when he had started throwing stones at a child smaller than he was. I, of course, intervened and told him that he could not do that. He replied by saying, "Well, you throw stones at me!" This was patently false, but so disturbed me, that I talked it over with the psychologist who had begun seeing Alec. The counselor told me that he had noticed that Alec tended to talk in metaphor. My having admonished Alec was interpreted by him as my having thrown stones. This gave me great pause as to how to handle him.

After nursery school, Alec moved onto a small private school run by a former college math professor who had become interested in the innovative teaching methods promoted by David Elkind, and had created an Open School. Fortunately, he had a well-trained staff to back him up because he had no experience at all in teaching children. The kindergarten teacher had a solid background in education, and later, Alec's upper grade teacher chose excellent materials from which each child could work individually at his or her own pace.

Alec was indifferent to the place though he did have an experience that he considered horrible. The kindergarten teacher, who should have known better, read to the class a story called "The Thing." It was about something ominous and black that waits outside the bedroom door. He didn't tell me about it at that time, but many years later he told me about how he would be in his room when we were having parties, as we did regularly every month, and that he would know the Thing was outside his door, and might come in at any minute, so he couldn't go outside the door to come on downstairs with guests. And so he would sit there and be terrified until the party was over, and then he could see his father or me and begin to feel safe. Clearly that one poem haunted his childhood.

Alec

Remember Mojo Risin' is right about them all: "You're all a bunch of fuckin' idiots!" (p1)

(Ed.: Alec is quoting Jim Morrison of The Doors who one time harangued an audience with: "Let people tell you what you're gonna do. Let people push you around. How long do you think its gonna last? How long are you gonna let it go on? How long are you gonna let them push you around. Maybe you love it. Maybe you like being pushed around. Maybe you love getting your face stuck in the shit.... You're all a bunch of slaves. Bunch of slaves. Letting everybody push you around. What are you gonna do about it? What are you gonna do about it.... What are you gonna do?")

I am a displaced child in this dying time. (19b)

In the land of the blind, the one-eyed man is killed as insane - ain't humans great? (32d)

Rooks and ravens are my cloak in the wind
the dead are my shadow, the dark is my path
beside me are demons, behind me is dust
dissolution springs under my tread
chaos, before me, unbound. (19d)

Litany to False Gods (#20)

Two spear litany of decay
Ten false gods lie dead today
The might of the mob has been proclaimed
Herd-psychology all to blame
Lock-step antichrist, autocracy
Fascistic endeavor, humanity
Tribal back broken - comes despair
Realization, genocide stare
Many weak hands rich in greed
Satisfying human kind's lifelong creed
Bearing down a world to a man-made fate
I am an animal, under this skin
I want to be fed, I want to breed
I won't admit it; I'll call it a sin
But all my religions honor this creed,
Give me security, give me my leisure
I'll live forever, I'll never die
Here are my lusts, provide for my pleasure
Don't make me think, my truth is a lie
I hate you more with every breath I draw

Reflection

I learned that Andria not only appreciated a well-educated mind, but she was highly engaged in the philosophy of education itself. Her college years, she remembered as one of the most cherished times of her life - free from an emotionally distant family to explore who she was and would be in the world, immersed in a world of ideas, surrounded by people who thrived on the ability to test their thoughts on one another, Andria was in heaven. I came to believe that she was an intellectual who, had she had greater self-confidence, or simply been born male, would likely have made a name for herself in academia. As it was, she took joy in sharing her passion for learning with her son, and was regularly frustrated by those to whom she entrusted his education. I have no doubt that some of the nonconformist, independent thought that she admired in Alec was a gift from her own DNA.

Children absorb so much in those first years of school. Aside from letters, numbers and colors, they are learning what is "normal" and how close or far off the mark they may be. Again, I think of my younger daughter who spoke more like an adult, and did not recognize teasing as a "normal" aspect of play, who had clear gifts in art, but drew with such detail that she could not fit into the "normal" time periods allotted for art projects to be completed. I think of the day that I got a call from the school because after the class had watched a film on MLK, Jr., the other children had gone out for recess while Naomi stayed behind crying because MLK, Jr. had been killed. I suspect that Andria, like me, had seen those aspects of her child that were outside of the curve as being their most remarkable traits, and had in some ways encouraged them.

Nonetheless, Alec began his school life much like most of us have - with blocks, paints, circle time, singing songs, show and tell, and stories read to try and settle the class down. And, like many of us, he developed a fear of the unknown - the Thing that might be waiting outside the door in the darkness. More profoundly, though, I suspect that he began to develop a sense of himself as somewhat outside of the norm, and, concurrently, somewhat suspicious of the norm.

It is challenging to look back from a place of knowing to a place of before-knowing. Alec was living with a nervous system that was wired differently than his peers, and his mind was already processing in a unique way - but, for all that, he was just a little boy.

Andria

The school concentrated a lot on bread baking, soup making, and these types of hands-on activities rather than on traditional academics, but that first year seemed satisfactory. The second year, unfortunately, the kindergarten teacher departed. The math professor took over the first and second grades and a new teacher was hired for the upper grades. The only qualifications she had that anyone could see was the fact that she was the headmaster's mistress, which was demonstrated all over the school, either when they were terribly fond of each other or terribly un-fond of each other. I grew increasingly dissatisfied with the quality of the academic work and the time they devoted to it. I visited for a whole day and discovered that they spent less than two full hours on academics, and that arithmetic was being taught by a parent who had never done so before and had no idea of the methodology of teaching. She was trying to teach the children about the lowest common denominator before she had even taught the principle of division. Alec's level (3rd-6th grades) had the most haphazard curriculum that ever was. The teacher made up the spelling list in the car on the way to school each day and there was very little regularity in the words. All the students learned the same material. There was no differentiation between what was taught to the third graders and what was taught to the sixth graders. All in all, it was an unholy mess, and I made the decision to move him out.

We visited our local public school and found it to be a warm and pleasant place. There were kids sitting on and under tables in the halls and wandering around. The principal's door was open and the children stuck their heads in to say hello as they passed by. The principal knew them all by name and was very pleased when students dropped in. The guidance counselor gave Alec a test, which demonstrated that this third grader was reading at a 12th grade level, and the principal was pleased at the idea of having Alec enroll.

Unfortunately, over the course of the summer, the principal departed for another state together with a woman teacher. With a lack of sanity that is still impressive, the school board appointed in his place a principal who had been removed from another elementary school by pressure from the parents. His only educational background was in adult education - a fact of which he was very proud. After he took over, the atmosphere of pleasantness was gone, replaced by rigidity and fear. In dealing with the children, they were thoughtless indeed. Alec, for instance, had started out in the lowest of the third grade math class because he had learned so little at his previous school and by sheer hard work he brought himself to the top of that class by Christmas. In January, they put him in the 4th grade class where he belonged, but this placed him at the bottom of the class again. This was just too discouraging for him to accept. He still did the work, but without very much enthusiasm.

There was a time when a book review was assigned and he asked permission to do _The Jungle Book_ by Rudyard Kipling. The teacher said, "No" because she didn't want short stories, she wanted one long full story. Alec explained that it was, in fact, a complete story, and she argued. He asked if he could bring the book in to show her and the teacher flatly refused. Instead, she told him to go find a good _Hardy Boys_ mystery. The idea of a 4th grade teacher having a student who could read and understand adult literature such as Kipling, but insisting on lesser fiction, was just too much for me and I yanked him from the school.

For a brief time, Alec was then enrolled in another private school that was governed by the tedious process of consensus. Selecting teachers for the consecutive year took from 2:00 in the afternoon until 2:00 in the morning for a decision to be made, and some of the choices were quite strange. The choice, for example, to fill a position for the upper level students was between a certified teacher who was very interested in the open school method of teaching, and a young woman whose only experience had been to be an assistant to the Kindergarten teacher at that school. There were people who thought that out of loyalty she should be appointed to the position regardless of the fact that she had no qualifications.

After a long time, the consensus was to get the certified teacher, which, as it turned out, was a fatal mistake - not because of the teacher, but because of the reaction of the parents. One family withdrew because they had lost the vote, and refused to allow their children to continue with the new teacher in place. Other parents were offended when they discovered that the teacher issued homework that she actually expected to be done. Gradually, throughout the year, it worked out very clearly that the majority of the children who attended this particular school were there because their parents did not want them to learn.

Alec

Reflection

Although the poem referenced by Alec's teacher was not kept, I was intrigued to find this note in a small folder of schoolwork saved by Andria. I can only imagine what goes through a teacher's mind when they read something by a student that has such evocative imagery. I wonder if they did talk together about this poem with its disturbing phrases? And, Andria - so much time committed to finding a school that would serve Alec's needs and gifts well. I particularly love this memory from Andria because it just captures her feisty insistence on quality, her determination to do right by her son, and the humorous turn of phrase that I so enjoyed when we would sit in her living room and talk. She was always able to tsk-tsk someone in a way that simultaneously recognized the inherent absurdity of the human condition.

Andria

Alec was fortunate in that the math teacher was first-rate, gentle, liked children and liked teaching math. She came to me one day and said that Alec puzzled her. She would teach him how to solve a given problem, then the proof for it, and then put forward a test problem to be solved silently by the students. Alec would return the paper with the answer correct and the proof valid, but it was not the proof she had taught him. He apparently was discovering mathematics on his own somehow. This independent operation of his mind was appreciated by this teacher, but not by many.

Alec

Mathematics communicates; The Mystery expresses (p2)

Kosko's Mathmaker in no way invalidates my idea of consciousness for chaos expressed through cosmos, indeed it bolsters it - Chaos to Mathmaker to Cosmos, but chaoticist vision skips the middleman/woman/creature and goes direct to chaos unrefined by chaologists and probability - math communicates, transcend to expression and ya get chaos. (p2)

Any fractal implies all things of which it is not fractal (the hologram is also mosaic) and more due to quantum indeterminacy. A fractal is never fixed, merely isolated from infinity, thus flux fractals. (16d)

...but fractal continuum - the music of life (12b)

I am a pataphysical fractal (p8a)

The One is also the None, thus 1x(ses) or the (N)ONE-8x(ses) - 0x(ses) ses = numbers what ain't ever been. (24d)

Science, religion, magic, mystic, whatever, all non-fractal. To answer a question raises at least one more question, which is fractal-growth-vide: Madelbrot set. By combining the Madelbrot set and the nirvana equation one has the formula of (Mystery) Freedom, add Sheldrake and CMT = Til Omnes Baphomet. (27d)

Chaologists measure probabilities between 0 and 1 - 0 since it can be conceived already possess a non-0 probability and 1 - certainty, which is self-negating. (31d)

Since 0 exists as probability there must have been SOME "awareness" around infinity to bring it into being - no first cause - various being simultaneously and otherwise - existing plank-to-plank (or whatever) - see above notes on 0 & 1 and conceptual reality. (32d)

The (universe - too small) whatever are simultaneous fractal geometries manifesting from primal Chaos following the Nirvana equation and corollaries and available via Azothic perception and are thus experiential, manipulable and affecting. (36d)

Khoronzon equation... if anything exists long enough to bootstrap itself (Crowley: I am, I am!)* mathematics occurs and, thusly, sheright! (40d)

Laser Light (#17)

Laser light
Cold steel and industrial machinery
Night
Hi-way passing far

Power ripping through
Tearing through the air
Pulls the breath from your lungs
Leaving the power in its place
Laser light
Percussion
Watch your thoughts crumble into dust
The moon runs away to hide
Unearth the fears and freedom
The meek crucified on raw energy
Power, peace
Each within the other
Each within you
Foreign control shattered
Impaled on the power
Sound of power, music for the spirit
Laser light
The chains are broken
Their shredded molecules glisten in
Laser light.

Reflection

I will have to leave judgment about Alec's use of mathematical concepts to someone more advanced in their understanding of fractals and probabilities, their interactions with physics, and their implications for chaos theory. What spoke to me in these passages was Alec's pleasure in taking these numerical thoughts and superimposing them on philosophical questions to derive some kind of rational, linear reasoning toward some unbounded, re-imagined future. Though I rarely grasped the details of his math-related entries, I could feel the "raw energy,""sound of power,""music for the spirit" as he rushed to record the thoughts surging through his mind.

Math as poetry in motion.

Andria

The school he was in closed down and fortunately, Harley accepted him. It was not a bad experience during the first couple of years. In fact, those two year of his life were probably the only ones in which he did what other people of his age did - he would go to

concerts at the War Memorial, and to
sleepovers at other young people's homes.

The interesting fact is that the parents liked
him to come by for visits. After he had spent
the night at one friend's house, the mother (who
was a shining example of grooming, good dress,
and a lot of money) went out of her way to tell
me that it was always so pleasant to have Alec
as a guest. The father of another student
remarked that he really enjoyed it when Alec
would come over because Alec got up as early
as did he, and while they had breakfast
together, they would talk. The man said it was
really like talking to another adult who was
just extremely pleasant company. Eventually,
Alec became uncomfortable at this particular
home, because his friend who lived there had
been adopted by this highly intelligent man and
his wife, but was himself only of average

intelligence. The mother had died, and Alec felt that the father had unreasonable expectations of his adopted son, and punished him for not doing better than he was capable of. Alec began to feel that the man was holding him up to his son in comparison, and making his friend feel worse.

By and large, Alec got on fairly well during the 5th and 6th grades. He particularly enjoyed being in the school plays. He had lead roles in both shows, having the unusual ability for someone of his age to remain in character even when he wasn't speaking. In one play, "You Can't Take it With You," they had transformed the drunken ballerina into a drunken ballet teacher, since apparently it was more palatable to the parents, they thought, for the drunk to be a male instead of a female. But Alec played a drunk beautifully, having watched the cast of MASH for a long time - and he had the speech and the mannerisms down well. He delighted the audience by staying in character for the curtain calls and swaying about, waving foggily at them with a soaked handkerchief. He genuinely enjoyed himself and performed well.

The next year they did another play, a much duller one, a useless sort of a thing, but he played the father of a family and it was interesting to see him, once again, embody the character throughout the performance. Somebody sitting behind me remarked at the end that he had been in two plays in two years and stolen both shows. This was perhaps putting it a little too strongly, but certainly he had brought a professional touch to his approach.

We had taken him to soccer games from the time he was in a stroller and had learned not to sit with the crowd because the noise they made when there was a goal scored was so tremendous that it terrified him. In retrospect, if I had known what kind of nervous system he had, I would never have taken him to those games, but nobody saw any sign of anything at that time.

We sat behind the goalpost where very few people sat and he watched soccer almost every Sunday for years, with the result that when he was seven and could play in Little League soccer, he went on that field and played like a natural player. He watched defenders because we were behind the goal, and he played right fullback just beautifully - his movements were skilled, his knowledge of the game was mature, his ability to dribble a ball was impressive. He could even do a sliding tackle without getting penalized. Alec knew how to pay attention - that's what his coaches discovered in Little League. He assimilated what he heard, and then put it into action. A coach once told me, "It's always nice to know that in that group there is one person who is listening to what I'm saying, and is going to put it into practice."

Alec (from folder of school work)

Let the faerie brands burn higher
Cleanse this evil place with fire.
Nothing shall remain to say
that evil here once had its way.
Let go the shimmering crimson flood
Which will bathe their souls in blood.
The evil which had held this place
Shall now give way to elven grace.
Let the ancient curse be sung
Upon these people shall it be hung.
Let the gods cleanse those fools
Of their mired, blemished rule.
Let the flames burn every higher
To create their funeral pyre.

Below is a story saved in Alec's school folder titled, "Book 2! Omenquest." Alec makes clear that many of the character names are taken from "Elfquest" by Richard and Wendy Pini, and that some of the creatures are drawn from Dungeons and Dragons created by Gary Gygax. In addition, please note that the parenthetical editorial notes are Alec's from the original pages.

Ripper found himself hustled along to a large building in the center of the village. "In you go!" yelled Treestump joyously. NightShade swallowed hard, said "(Censored)," quietly under his breath and allowed himself to be shoved in.

At first, Ripper saw nothing. The reason for that

was because his eyes were closed, but finally he opened them. He gasped. He saw an Elf - a female Elf - but a <u>tall</u> female Elf, fully 5'6" tall. She was the most beautiful Elf that could be imagined!

"Uh, hello," said NightShade.

"Hello," she said, her voice was soft. "Come closer."

NightShade took 3 steps forward.

"What is your name?" she asked.

"NightShade," he replied.

"I am Savah," she said.

"Well, uh, hello."

"Oh!" she cried.

"What is it, Savah?" cried Cutter.

"I sense incredible power," she cried, "coming from him!" pointing to NightShade.

"What type of power?" cried Skywise.

"I don't know," she said, "but it is incredible!"

"Come, NightShade," said Cutter. "Savah needs rest."

"All right."

"Do you know what your power is?" said Skywise.

"Yes."

"What?"

"Fruit ripening."

"Fruit ripening?"

But before he could say more, they were flocked by oohing, aahing, and giggling villagers.

"Stop!" yelled Cutter.

"Let's celebrate our visitor's arrival with a party," said Skywise.

"Yes! Yes!" screamed the villagers.

Approximately an hour later, everyone was outside the village and was drinking, eating, and dancing. Everyone was happy.

Then it happened. While nobody was armed, it happened.

There was a scream and a yell and down plunged large, heavy, lumbering humanoids.
"What are they?" yelled Skywise.
"Hobgoblins!" yelled NightShade.
"Goblin guts!" (good line.)

Reflection

After spending months in the journals that Alec kept during the last few years of his life, it was such a breath of fresh air to pause and open the slim folder of Alec's schoolwork that Andria had saved. Here was a poem sounding like it belonged firmly in the Tolkien tradition. And, here was a story written by Alec, mimicking the literature he already loved, enjoying the process of filtering known characters through his own imagination, and dipping his toes into the titillating possibilities posed by attractive females, while censoring himself (something he never did in his adult writings.) Not only was it satisfying to catch this glimpse of a young, less jaded Alec, but to be able to smile with a mother's smile at his creative efforts. How can you read this short passage and not grin when he notes at the end: ("good line.") It's a keeper.

Andria

When I look back on that period, I realize that he very rarely brought home from school good news, good tales of what happened that day. Occasionally he did, as when the music teacher on 6th or 7th grade played Ives, and Shostakovich, Gershwin's Rhapsody in Blue - unusual music with which he was absolutely delighted. This was the first indication that he was tremendously interested in music. He had been brought up with classical music all around him because that's all that was ever on the radio.

It was interesting that even when he was quite small certain things would bother him that you wouldn't expect to. We had a record with Haydn's "Toy Symphony" on it and a surprise ending on the other side. The "Toy Symphony" he liked immensely, but the surprise ending he would tell me not to play. He would grow agitated if I put it on. Again, in retrospect, the surprise elements, the quietness followed by the loud sounds in that recording startled him, and he wasn't comfortable with it, and didn't want any part of it.

His age-mates had reached the phase of pushing, pulling, tugging, punching and whatnot, and he disliked this a great deal. On one occasion he came home from school to report that some kid had punched him the arm as he went by and Alec had stopped him, really smoking mad. His anger had surprised the other guy completely because the boy was just behaving normally. Still, with that kind of behavior, I wasn't sure if he was in the right situation.

He was the odd man out at this school. At private schools with expensive fees, children tend to be very well dressed, but Alec liked to wear jeans, a jean jacket and a tshirt - not at all the "in thing" to do and, as usual, he didn't give a damn. He was going to dress the way he wanted to dress and if somebody didn't like it, it was their tough luck.

By the time he was halfway through 8th grade, Alec was getting violent, and becoming increasingly anti-school. In fact, the truth is, he was threatening to blow up the school and machine gun down teachers, kill students, horrible things like that. I gushed with a psychologist who worked with him who said, "You get him out of that school or you'll ruin him."

Alec

As a revolutionary every action one takes is by definition a revolutionary act. (2b)

Plurals are a lingual time saver, plurality a conceptual short cut and rule of thumb. All is unique and a singularity unto itself. (3b)

The one thing stronger than hatred or forgiveness is not giving a flying fuck. (13b)

A friend is just an enemy on a waiting list. (21b)

(from folder of school work – Grade 7):

A cloak of sable hung around an ivory moon.
The muted patter of rain sounded upon leaves and the olive steel of my helmet.
The ashen drops of rain glistened on the domed helmets of my comrades
I sat in a muddy hole, not moving for fear of unseen death.
The rain fell softly, making no noise, unlike the loads of steel and explosive that came daily.
I look upon my weapon, gleaming darkly. I have come to look upon it as my friend
It is a sorry time when this must happen.

I glance upon my watch, seventeen hundred hours it reads.

Soon my enemies will be emerging from the virgin light of day.

And even now as death approaches, I am calm.

For now I sit and contemplate the beauty of the dawn.

Reflection

It fascinated me that as often as Andria related this part of Alec's story to me, she always told it the same way. She always quoted the psychologist as telling her to remove Alec from that school "or you will ruin him." Andria freely talked about Alec's growing violence, telling me that she bought him a steady supply of cheap crockery that she kept in the garage for those times when he needed to act on his aggression and smash something. And, she was aware of his threatening thoughts toward his school, teachers and classmates. But, the climax of the tale was always this warning from the psychologist to remove Alec from the school before IT ruined HIM. Perhaps Andria understood the counselor to mean that if Alec acted on his thoughts, it would not only harm those around him, but ruin his life as well. Perhaps, but it is not how I heard her as she would remember these words being spoken. I believe that Andria saw the continuing attempt to channel Alec through the traditional route of adolescence would somehow destroy the person he was meant to be. Even in his most frightening moments of imagined and real violence, his mother saw the uniquely valuable and vulnerable child deserving of his own path.

Alec wrote, "Viewpoints don't shift, people shift in relation to their views." (36d)   As is often true in life, those of us on the outside judge without knowing, assessing behaviors, words, appearances from our own perspective, without access to that which lies beneath the surface. It wasn't until I had known Andria for some time that she shared with me some of the difficult realities of her life, and, by extension, Alec's....

Andria

During most of his childhood, Alec was living in an atmosphere of stress. It was my hope that because he was so small, he would not feel it to any great degree. I had been, myself, badly mothered and had no natural instinct for it. For the first few years of my life, I was left in the care of a nursemaid and during that time, the maid's boyfriend raped me - something I didn't tell anyone until I was in detox shortly after graduating college. I was close to my father, however, and named Alec after him.

My relationship with his sister, Kate, who was named after the heroine in Henry V, began to deteriorate immediately after Alec was born. He required a great deal of energy and attention, and she felt resentful toward him - a feeling that only grew throughout her lifetime. It was certainly in part my fault. Kate was already having a rough time in school and I leaned on her a little too much after Alec came along, until one day, Kate said, "Mom, I'm only eleven!" I stopped asking after that, and we stopped talking.

For reasons no one could understand at the time, by the time Alec was six months old, his father's behavior began to change dramatically. Jerry always had been good humored, civil and courteous, and now he became very depressed looking, very tired. Frequently he was far less than civil or thoughtful and more likely to be sarcastic and critical - not to any great degree and not to where a very small child would understand it, but it did make me angry because I saw no reason for such behavior. Though I still had extraordinary respect for his intellect and his work as an anthropologist/linguist, the affection was long gone.

Jerry was terrible to his teenage daughter. It seemed to all indication that as she developed from a little girl into a teenager, he experienced great sexual sensation towards her. He requested that she not wear baby doll pajamas around the house, but to wear a kimono over them. At one point, he kissed her with enthusiasm on the lips, which she told him made her uncomfortable. Hereafter, he never approached her physically.

Aside from his confusing relationship with Kate, I believed that Jerry was also engaged in a homosexual relationship with a man over the course of months.

His way of handling any situation he found emotionally challenging was to withdraw. He felt that people who gave way to their emotions were weak and were just not of strong character. Weeping or crying when something had gone wrong was thoroughly disapproved of and this had a disastrous effect on his children.

While all this was going on Alec was growing up a good deal used to it. His father didn't come home until about 5:00, and then after playing and talking with Alec for a while, he would start reading the evening paper, have dinner, go up to bed, stay until 11:00pm, get back up, work a while, and then go back to bed. He'd be asleep when Alec went off to nursery school. So, really, Alec only saw his father about a half an hour a day, and a little more on the weekends, which was probably just as well due to the negative behaviors his father displayed. His habit of withdrawing affection as a sign of showing disapproval would have been very tough. It was certainly tough on Kate.

One morning, when Alec was five years old, he came downstairs and discovered his father lying in a pool of blood. In fact, blood was everywhere. Jerry had had a cerebral hemorrhage, and had died almost immediately. Kate had already left for school, and my first and only thought was to remove Alec from the scene, so I called a neighbor who came and took him to school, believing that his father had had an accident with cranberry juice. The funeral parlor came and cleaned up the living room, so that there was no sign of the incident when the children returned from school. Kate went to her room, and Alec very calmly and rationally said, "He can't be dead. I need a father."

Alec

People after extreme trauma will often recall the oddest or tiniest things with exact detail, and will often comment on "I remember specifically..." - akin to epiphany. (39d)

A blues arising and giving wordless voice to the scream that echoes inside us but is heard by none, shared by all: a blues of alienation, angst, existential despair, the trance of sorrow. (16b)

Reflection

As a minister, I am privy to information about people's lives that some of their closest friends and even family members may not know. I recognize on any given Sunday that while I am looking out upon the tidy group before me thumbing through their hymnals, that underneath their polished appearance is a seething mass of issues, sorrows, troubled marriages, lost children, bitter memories, confused thoughts, addictions, loneliness, and secrets. I have learned to leave a little room around each person's words and actions for that hidden self to reside. Some days I'm better at it than others.

From the perspective of such distance, it is easy to feel a deep sympathy for Alec as I struggle to imagine what his days were like - living with a nervous, anxiety disorder that sent adrenaline through him, causing his mind and nervous system to race non-stop, while living in a household of disordered relationships, magnified and further distorted by the sudden, explosive death of the father. In fact, it's hard to imagine how Alec could have functioned normally in the world given this burden. Would I have had the insight to recognize this, however, if I were the mother of one of his classmates as he threatened to destroy them? Would I have admired his nonconformist individuality if it directly impacted me and my life? Will I recognize the complexity behind the next odd, abrasive, intimidating, off-putting person that I meet?

Andria

So, I began to make preparations to remove him from school. It was a rather sad time to do it because his social science class had just gone through a lesson in which they staged a debate with formal teams. Alec had, of course, been chosen last for a group and they had each taken their turn until, finally, it was his turn. Since he was highly verbal and organized, his closing arguments went very well, and he made a very effective speech. His teacher later in the day went past me and said, "You're bringing up a lawyer, you know that!" I didn't know what he meant until I asked Alec about it at home. He smiled wryly and said though he'd been chosen last, he figured he'd pretty well impressed them. The next day he was asked to be captain of the team, a rare affirmation that he enjoyed.

The school was, by this time, recognizing Alec's intelligence and was unhappy with my taking him out. It was the soccer coach, though, that asked me to come to his office. He had heard I was thinking of taking Alec out of school and begged me not to do it because they had waited for two years for him to be able to join the

Junior Varsity team. I was astonished because, as I said to the coach, "He can't run that fast and he can't make his man - he just feels it."

The coach said it didn't matter because Alec knew the game. He always understood where he should be, and was always ahead of what was going to happen. I felt badly because Alec enjoyed playing soccer and he wouldn't have another chance, but it was too important a decision to hang on a future possibility in soccer.

We began homeschooling, having Alec work with a series of tutors who were, by and large, a waste of time. He had one tutor who was supposed to teach him a course in sociology and who ended up having him just read the Constitution aloud, which was really sort of pitiable. So that was canceled.

He had another history teacher who taught not history and not facts, but his opinion of history and facts. Instead of teaching about a Supreme Court decision, he would simply say if he thought it was right or wrong as a kind of flat statement of fact. I objected to this approach and found myself listening to the tutorials and then going back and correcting all the misinformation he had managed to convey.

Likewise, we were unable to find an adequate math teacher, and ended up going to a special "learning center" where he worked with the head of the organization. After 3 sessions with her, she came out saying that his only problem with math was that he was too good at it. Alec was later tested by a specialist who came to the conclusion that his mind just worked so fast on math problems that he was unable to say how he arrived at the answers.

Ultimately, he took his GED and passed it
without any difficulty.

This could have been Stanley M. in fact Harpur entered at age 14 - 13 in fact switched majors. took at 16 y.o. of age 19 yr. old young woman! to a formal. Wow! years rest As

Alec

I read/watch/cite material that is counter to my ideas
and revise my ideas when I am proved wrong - 8th grade
and a GED, I do this. Nobel prize winners do not - so
FUCK 'EM! (5c)

The path is the goal
The question is the answer
To seek is to find
The chase is the catch
The means are the ends
There are no ends, only means. (37d)

Reality (laws) are a self-generated lattice of crystal
laws imprisoned in a globe of faith. Smash the crystal!
Til Omnes Baphomet! Sherite! (12b)

History is subject to revisionism, the memory has been
proven faulty in scientific studies and court cases.
Brainwashing, whether by media or torture comes into
play. The future is only determined by thoughts and
WILL. Any predicted or pre-ordained events may be
subverted. Chaos Theory, Quantum mechanics, the

illusion of linear time (retro E. and linear time applies to memory.) Both history (H) and the future (F) are available to anyone who will embody chaos and open himself to info. At the quantum level (meaning leaving ego/possibly self-definition) and even then the definitions are most likely to be made consciously. Thus memory history and future are subjective, being defined by the strongest will, or ignored (or taken as object lessons) by those who feel emancipated by chaos, as opposed to fearing it and naming it evil. Thusly, the truth taking stare means facing the ultimate responsibility (no Randist shit or Libertarian shit); playing the hand that's dealt as opposed to nursing at the cancerous tit of anyone or any "-ology." (8d)

Village Warm-up (#9)
Ol' peg-leggedy lizard

Some electricity, dilapidated powerlines,
ancient small generator run by a young gnome
who inherited it from his father and so on for
generations.
Bar has a fridge, generator dies at least once a day.
The Mayor has one telephone, and the chief of police
the other.
Both are inherited posts.
There is one constable.

The whorehouse has a pinball machine.

The bar is the only one anywhere that can advertise

"cold draft beer" in the window

any season besides winter.

The whorehouse sells dirty postcards drawn by the parson

to pay for the vestry roof

beneath which he sleeps in a tent.

The local sorcerer is a transvestite

and will charge less for his services

if you call him "Glinda."

Reflection

I almost feel sorry for those who came forward to tutor Alec. Between his mental capacity for juggling ideas, for deconstructing arguments and formulating alternate conclusions, and his mother's high standards for the teaching profession, it was a challenging role to fulfill - and very few did. As Andria listened in on sessions so that she could debrief her son later, she guaranteed that Alec would adopt this questioning stance toward everything he would hear and learn thereafter. The one thing, which is made clear through his journals, is that Alec craved learning, but resisted accepting what he learned as any kind of final truth. Even those authors he most admired were challenged in his journals, while at the same time, inviting challenges to his own thinking as well.

This book was almost titled, "Til Omnes Baphomet!" as it was one of Alec's favored phrases. Ultimately, though, I had to conclude that even fewer people would think to pick up and browse through a book with such an arcane title. More importantly, and more honestly - if I chose this phrase as the title, it would suggest that I believed it somehow captured the essence of Alec's writings, and here I would need to be honest in admitting that I never fully understood his use of these three words. Though his meaning remains stubbornly obscure, I am nearly certain that Alec has adopted the figure of Baphomet from the writings of Aleister Crowley, a British occultist whose books were among Alec's most cherished, and well-thumbed resources. If anyone were to be led to explore Alec's thinking on a deeper level, Crowley would be required reading. Crowley's spiritual philosophy, known as Thelema, had at its core the belief that individuals should claim and pursue their own True Will - not to be determined by others, or by any existent law or moral code. This True Will was not to be confused with momentary wants and desires, but by an overarching life purpose, which, when discovered, would align oneself with the forces of the universe. Baphomet, often confused with Satan as depicted in Tarot, represents the harmonious conjunction of cosmic dualities:

"This serpent, SATAN, is not the enemy of Man, but He who made Gods of our race, knowing Good and Evil; He bade 'Know Thyself!' and taught Initiation. He is 'The Devil' of the Book of Thoth, and His emblem is BAPHOMET, the Androgyne who is the hieroglyph of arcane perfection... He is therefore Life, and Love. But moreover his letter is "ayin," the Eye, so that he is Light; and his Zodiacal image is Capricornus, that leaping goat whose attribute is Liberty." (Aleister Crowley, Magick: Book 4, pg. 51)

I include this brief bit of research only because Crowley's writings had a clear influence on Alec's thinking during his last few years of life, giving shape and flavor and imagery to much of Alec's inner inclinations. Each time Alec would punctuate his own journaled thoughts with "Til Omnes Baphomet," it was with the sense of a door slammed on the limited thinking of others, and a passionate outburst of hope - hope in a future defined by the coming together of dualities, a chaos bound through intent of the will, each person's mortality interwoven with a recognition of each one's divinity. Finally, Crowley also used Baphomet to symbolize the "magical child" created by the joining of opposites. Alec was forever, at his core, a magical child.

Andria

I wasn't worried about his general education. We had a large, excellent library at home, public broadcasting was a great resource, and so at that point was the channel called "Arts & Entertainment," which frequently produced plays, or rather the films of plays, as they were being done on Broadway. We met up with some really marvelous ones. Alec's favorite was Richard Friar Bailey's work, "This Witch is Not for Burning" which is a tremendous play. Alec was also fond of a George Bernard Shaw play that I had never heard of and which was not in my _Complete Works of George Bernard Shaw_ volume either, but that was great fun. We taped a lot from that channel.

In addition, he would watch new and different things. PBS was doing an occasional historical documentary on England, which fed into Alec's interest in knights in armor, castles and such. He had spent time studying Greek and Roman soldiers, their tactics of warfare and siege, and perhaps these documentaries fitted in with that. I have no idea, but he seemed to have watched them and absorbed them.

Alec

Mab's voice and the voice of my DA are the same in quality - a harmony of malevolence. (p1)

If I can call Mab to my side (she who may have given me life), then she can counsel me on life "issues." My birth was unlikely - perhaps she helped? (27b)

The next evolution may need a curse to kick off and I am here to provide it with my unusual (Into the Woods) enlightenment should conventional enlightenment fail. Witch: "I'm not good, I'm not nice, I'm just right." (4b)

Reasonably regarded, the witch is very much like me in action and motivation - the witch and I are one. (5b)

Matrix of Pain (#1)

Construct of life

Suffering

A verity

Nowhere to flee

For your path is part of the matrix

Denial the choice of those who would pluck their own eyes

Striving not to cause pain

Your life is a strand in the matrix

Others will suffer because of your life

Others because you have left it

Death is a strand in the matrix

No hiding

No running

No dying

No hope

Now I have no place to live

You have turned me out

I can find no place to live

People, turn away.

Reflection

Throughout Alec's journals, he periodically references Mab (a powerful goddess from the TV series, Merlin, which he much enjoyed), as well as the witch portrayed by Bernadette Peters in the broadcast version of "Into the Woods." They seem to represent an aspect of his identity on a more mythological plane - one which I think it is safe to say was often more real to him than the mundane "truths" of his existence. Drawn to these feminine archetypes, Alec responded to their insistence on living their power into the midst of their circumstances, without concern for the moral implications declared by others. "I'm not good, I'm not nice, I'm just right." These words from the play rang true in his life. One can argue that he rationalized his own impulses toward the "not good" and "not nice" by believing himself to be meant for something that made human approval of him unlikely, but was nonetheless "right." Likewise, it would be easy to psychoanalyze his mother issues as revealed by these choices of role models. I think it may even be possible that his interest in these characters was provoked by the attractive actresses who portrayed them. But, again, throughout Alec's journals, I believe that he found his deepest sense of identity through a combination of myth and physics leading him to see his destiny as one that would transpire on some cosmic scale, beyond this particular space/time continuum.

Andria

By this time, he had discovered what was to be
his real life, which was the world of music. I
took him to the local music store, which had
both instruments and lessons and was just
under a mile away. He began studying guitar,
and this was extremely difficult for him, as he
did not like to do anything in front of people
until he could do it well. But to learn guitar,
you have to practice and do it in front of people
who can correct you, and at first he made very
little progress. He began to have doubts, but I
was convinced he could do it and told him so and
bought him a very expensive guitar he'd been
admiring.

Alec was fortunate to have a perceptive
teacher. It quickly became clear that Alec
hated repetition and that if he had to play a

scale ten times, the teacher quickly decided that the tenth time would be worse than the first. So, he very cleverly mixed up the lessons. They'd play scales, then some rhythm, some harmony, and do some theory. By keeping it varied in this way, Alec began to learn, and then, suddenly everything gelled and it all came together. At one point, the proprietor of the shop said that nobody in the place had thought that Alec would ever play the guitar and then, six months later, they were bragging about this marvelous guitarist they had on their hands.

By the time he was 17, people were trying to make use of him. There was one jazz guitar man in the city who wanted to promote a trio in which Alec would be the lead guitar. The man around the music shop wanted to produce some recordings where Alec would write the arrangements and then would be assisted in the studio. It turned out that the band players thought the arrangements were too difficult and they couldn't handle them. So, the agreement was that Alec would play all the string parts and just dub them in one after another. That was the way it was left, but the proprietor of the shop changed his mind. The head of the original band, who had no virtue except that he had a four-octave voice of not tremendous quality, decided that his band would try and play the old arrangement after all. Alec discovered this quite by accident and said, "Well then you do it." He wanted no part of it. The proprietor, who was a very macho man, and could never afford to be beaten by anybody, said that was "unprofessional." So, Alec showed up, spent his time with the producers and the electronic people, learned a lot and enjoyed himself, but had nothing to do with the recording. Later the proprietor played the recording at the shop and declared that he was going to send it to a friend of his as proof of his own producing abilities. Alec told him he could send it anywhere he liked, but to make sure his name wasn't on it. And that was the end of that particular episode in the music department.

Alec rarely showed off his abilities on the guitar - he didn't feel any need to compete with other people. In fact, one of his specific desires was to avoid sounding like anybody else. He once made a tape of his own work, which I played for a friend who said she saw, or heard echoes of Bartok and Miles Davis, and of other people who had influenced him. When I reported this to Alec, he simply discarded the tape. He didn't want anything that showed signs of derivation from somebody else's work.

Occasionally, he did try to play with other people, and at one point put a trio together. It was to be a very experimental affair where a bassist, drummer and guitarist play at the same time, but not together - each playing whatever he wanted to without reference to what the others were doing. The trio was noted for the competency of the players, each of them were individually excellent and their music had a certain appeal that I really enjoyed. They played out, just once, at a club where the performance was videotaped and recorded at the same time, but Alec was not happy with the results and erased the tape. After about six months, Alec dissolved the group having become less and less interested in playing with other people and more and more comfortable totally on his own.

During the next years, he enjoyed the nights when he had the house to himself and recorded over 200 cassettes worth of music, along with reel to reel tapes, all of which were transcribed onto CD after his death with some posted to the website.

That was the most satisfactory period of his life. He was provided the equipment that he needed because I had set up the education fund which was now a music fund, and I drew upon that to buy him whatever was necessary for his playing and composing. I'm glad he had those five years of immersion in music because that's something he left behind as a legacy and because it was, I think a happy time for him, and probably the only happy time he had in his life.

Alec

(Margin note - p.3): get digital watch with stopwatch for recording.

START MUSIC! Avenge through art. (p8a)

margin note: band name 12th Night (p9a)

Record 4-track to 88 to CD - relax (6c)

When ya can PLAY silence, then you're happening. (6c)

Guitar licks are like lines from playwright - it is who plays/speaks that defines profundity from mediocrity. (85d)

Reflection

In keeping with Alec's will toward freedom, and embrace of chaos, his music reflects both. Perhaps even more than the written word, one comes closest to "knowing" Alec by experiencing his music. Some of his compositions and recordings were captured in CD form, and can be heard (and ordered from) his website: www.alecwilliams.com.

Andria

It wasn't just that Alec withdrew from others, they withdrew from him as well. It was noticeable in the music store. If Alec were looking through the LPs, on either side of him, there would be at least a foot of vacant space. He gave off some sort of aura that said, "I don't want anybody too close to me." The only person in the shop who ignored this was a very buff Irishman who would come in and clap Alec on the shoulder. Alec would simply, if he saw the man coming, move to avoid him. Alec talked to the other musicians, but he didn't socialize with patrons in general, and they didn't attempt to socialize with him.

This reminds me of a time when Alec was waiting for a school bus when he was very young. A large black dog, a gentle creature used to playing with the school children, came down the path toward them wagging its tail, looking pleased to see a young person. Alec, who was terrified of dogs, having had a frightening experience with a German shepherd when he was very small, stared at the dog and at least five yards from them, the dog stopped dead in his tracks and backed away, his tail between his legs.

As his hair got longer and he continued to wear all black, he became a somewhat off-putting sight as well. Elderly people, in particular, were nervous around him. We were riding an elevator one day with a very small old lady in it. She was obviously apprehensive about Alec. He could sense her anxiety, and casually lifted the book he was carrying so that she could see that he was "the kind of person who read books." Despite his appearance, which he intentionally created to look fierce and dangerous, Alec was always soft-spoken, articulate, and polite to those with whom he did interact.

One time, we were involved in a minor car accident. It was winter and the car we were following slid in front of us. Alec said, "I think we're going to hit that car." I said, "I think we are too." And we did. I went into a nearby house to ask if I might use the phone to call the police. The woman very kindly let me in. A moment later, Alec came to the door, and to my surprise she opened the door to him as well. He was not the sort of person that you would think someone would let through the door, but his speech was soft and that of an educated person. He had spoken very politely saying that I was his mother and he just needed to speak with me for a moment. His essential gentleness had shown through. And, despite his fear of dogs, when I decided to rescue two Sheltie puppies from an abusive home, he put up with it. He very often put up with things because they gave me pleasure.

Alec

Despite my increasingly negative and isolative outlook, the vibes I send out unconsciously seem to have a more beneficial / positive effect on those I meet. (8b)

Immolation (#2)

Make the outside like the inside

Set myself aflame

Flame outpouring from my eyes,

Igniting all I see

Hatefulness alight inside me,

Blackened flesh within

All outside anathema,

Burn it all away

Scorch the Earth that is outside,

So no outside can live

I am in possession of the power

I am the alchemist of Man.

Reflection

We so often move through the world unaware of our impact. While each of us is, in fact, the star of our own story, numerically speaking, our lives are most often measured by the times we are merely an "extra" in the stories of others. Sometimes we get to co-star for a period of time, or play some pivotal role in the plot, but often, we are just background noise in other people's worlds. I will sometimes pause to wonder how many times I appear in other people's photo albums as just a random face in the crowd. Alec is now forever one of those characters who has passed through the pages of my life... and yours.

Andria

Because he was a night person, he did all his musical work at night. We had an L-shaped living room, and that L part of it was to be his area for his music gear. The floor was frequently so covered with cords that he had to tiptoe through it. Even his 25-pound cat, Zappo, who went wherever Alec went, walked with great caution among all those cords.

Gradually, as his equipment needs increased,

he began to outgrow the L shape and sort of flowed into the rest of the living room. I took refuge in the dining room, where I was perfectly comfortable.

Alec wanted a number of guitars because each one would perform a special function. Since I liked buying guitars, I had no trouble with that. He also liked all kinds of equipment, which we had a little discussion over because I called them little black boxes and he called them musical instruments. It was a friendly kind of difference and caused no trouble between us. He did not like to handle business so I became the business manager. He told me what he needed and then I would call up the music store we were dealing with and either purchase it or order it to be delivered. Alec had originally gone into the store himself and had been very comfortable there, but as his desire grew to be alone, as his paranoia increased, even that place became a source of anxiety. But the storeowner liked Alec and his playing a great deal, so he would let me take a guitar home for Alec to try out with no money down. More often than not, I would call the next day and ask how much, and then send him a check.

Alec

I am absurd, such is a dragon's nature; I am a fool, alone and knowing what only a fool can see, such is the nature of a fool. Solitude and senses of unusual kind serve both and so myself. The Western Dragon is beyond dadaist. (p2)

Dragons and fools (of which I am both) see and sense what others cannot and thus are solitary in absurdity cynicism. (16c)

I shall be not satisfied with having less than art - and human relationships ain't even close, so come not near me. (7c)

Lesson fer tonight: you are what yo is; no point trying to change it or convert anyone to your path. Yes, you are evil. (25b)

Gods are just people who make their dreams real. Refuse limitation and it gets discouraged. (28b)

Berlin Wall (#12)

Slate grey overhead
And underneath our feet
Lidded eyes and moistened lips
Fingers brush nipple under silk
Soft sounds lapping at my ears
I smell dust and rust and you
These tired eyes would close without you
Standing on the Berlin Wall

Bass line (solo) end on open A harmonic
Silent 4 ct
Bass + drums (guitars swell in)
Spoken word
Solo/bass to drums wander a bit
Return to original riff - Fade

Reflection

"Refuse limitation and it gets discouraged." This line stopped me in my tracks the first time I read it. I wrote it down in the margin of my own notebook, and later put it on a sticky note to attach to my computer at work. The idea of limitation as something outside of me trying to impose itself on my life, has shaken me loose more than once. And the idea that Alec - who was by all reasonable measures, severely limited by his own circumstances - refused to surrender to those limits is a humbling reminder that whatever outside (or inside) forces seem to be me holding me back are only there because I have allowed them to stay. Refuse limitation and it gets discouraged. Refuse limitation and it gets discouraged. Refuse limitation...

Andria

As mentioned before, Alec had a tendency toward violence. At one time, early on, a psychologist gave Alec a Rorschach test. Alec's responses scared the psychologist, who called and scared me. I witnessed his anger on occasions, and eventually began stocking cheap crockery in the garage so that when he needed to, he could go out and smash things. He didn't want to learn how to drive a car because he thought he might start using it as a weapon. When a psychic asked him why he hated people so much, he said it was because they weren't what they could be.

Alec

Like the Aliens in "Lathe of Heaven," only unholy opposition will cause humanity to bond together and become more than it is. My gig seems to be adversary (Satan - if ya wanna be biblical), rejected, dejected but I will not be ashamed. (p1)

I know what I am, beyond Ipsissimus, when I say I, I mean beyond god - no more fucking around and nobody fucks with me. No more locking down, let it loose. Sherite! (7a)

Til Omnes Baphomet - Let the good times roll (2b)

A dark side must exist, if only to drive people beyond complacency and niceness. Dark win or lose is unimportant, the resistance it offers is its importance. (22b)

Living as non-scumbags is easiest, but the rules we impose as laws inhibit us from nonscumbag behavior. (32d)

The will-to-kill is needed - it is wanting and wishing to kill that creates scumbags. (33d)

<u>Iron Frost</u> (#21)

Locked doors

Squeezed into corners to pray

Fear

Its breath fills every brain

All await

The Iron Frost

Outside all dies

With never a chance of decay

Frozen In moment of death

By rusted fist of frost

Resistance

Useless

Surrender - no terms

Merely await extinction

By evening

All will die

Felled by

The Iron Frost

Our world an abattoir

No war

This is the end

Unstoppable

Soon there will be only dust

To mark the passing of

The Iron Frost

Reflection

We meet Alec through the quieted pages of his journals -
gentled by time and distance. His mother's anxiety at the
sound of dishes being hurled against walls, softened and
soothed in retrospect. As I work my way through this task -
this holy effort - to preserve the voice of one who walked
this earth, I am increasingly aware of how my own
struggles, joys, heartbreaks, emotions, actions, regrets,
plans, questions, beliefs, memories - will be flattened with
time into a one-dimensional impression left along the way:
"Frozen in moment of death." Alec's words and Andria's
remembrances take on substance only as they are
absorbed into each of our hearts, interacting with our own
experiences of life, melted and re-crafted in our own image.

Andria (and daughter, Kate)

Alec's life became very upset at one point when I discovered that my ophthalmologist had not treated my glaucoma properly, and then I'd lost a great deal of my sight and could no longer drive. I was the only driver in the family, and our house was not within walking distance of shops or doctors, so we had to move. He was 21 when I entered two years of deep depression and heavy drinking.

My first impulse was to move us near to the University of Chicago, which I had always loved. Kate, who was living there at the time, chose a condo for us. It was lovely, but was not - as it turned out - any more workable than our home had been in Rochester. In addition, Alec and I discovered that Kate had become an alcoholic and was not at all pleasant to be near.

We needed to put some physical distance between us.

After we returned to Rochester, to a new house, I checked myself into Strong and dealt with my own drinking. Unlike Kate, I was able to regain control of my use of alcohol, and my life. Years later, I asked Alec, "Was I as mean as Kate was?" His reply: "No. You weren't much fun to be with, but you were never mean."

I spent about six months going back and forth to tend to Kate who was on disability leave from her job because of her drinking. This was hard on Alec, who didn't like to be alone, but he tolerated it as best he could.

Eventually, I moved Kate to Rochester because I could no longer handle the commute. At this point, Alec became actively unhappy, with every reason to be. His sister was intent upon making his life as miserable as possible. Gradually, I had to forbid her entrance to the house, not let her have a key, not let her come over between certain hours. We often didn't even answer the phone. But, she learned to call late at night, which she knew was the time when I left the house to Alec. In general, it was a demanding and extremely difficult period for him and I should have handled it better, but I did the best I could at the time and it wasn't nearly sufficient.

Alec

re: Kate and "get over it" - I respect that ultimately she must help destroy herself with the same options I have for, like me, traditional med. has and will continue to fail. (p3)

Kate has succeeded in driving a wedge between my mother and myself. (14b)

Since before my birth, Kate's main drive (conscious, unconscious, or probably both) has been to vandalize, mutilate, and if possible, destroy relations between myself and my mother - Kate's slow death should be recognized as a last desperate ploy to that end - I suspect she will manage to live as long as one of the pair of us does, simply to get the job done. This is her WILL. Death is merely a means to an end. (15b)

These difficulties (2 hour conversations, offers on my part to split, screaming shakes) wouldn't exist if you hadn't brought Kate home. It ain't easy being yer father's daughter? DUTY! It's worse being yer father's daughter's son! After-affect fucks one up. Even honest attempts at well-doing are blown because understood in duty/shitbag terms. Fuck ya! (17b)

I am tired of being thought stupid when others are mired. The same goes for putting up with others' temper when I have conceptually pressed them, and I am tired of being called evil because I am HONEST - an unwholesome reminder. I am my own sacrifice. All I need to remember Mordred's sentiment is my father/sister. (30b)

Mom: in 2 births poison has been brought out. 1, a poison to man (Kate), the other a poison of god (Sammael) - the first to cause strife, the second to realize its ending (so I hope.) (5c)

Kate: Betty Boop at Betty Ford's (6c)

Blades (#4)

You use words like men use knives
I use knives like you use words
Let me speak to you
(I want to speak to you)

The tongue that cleaves
The blade that leaves a scar

When your lips are closed
And my shank is sheathed
Perhaps there will be peace

Blood of the brain
Blood of the flesh
Equal wounds

Left unbound we're left with scars
That time will not erase

(sound)

bass and tone drums riff1 - 12x - vox after 2x

drum fill - 4ct

bass+drum riff2 - 8x - vox after 1x

solo

b+d riff1 - 2x

d fill 4 ct

b+d riff2 - 1x - resolve to A

(sound)

Reflection

Ahh, Kate. How I wish I knew more about Kate. What was her story? How would she have written Alec's story? Andria never spoke to me much about Kate. I think that in some ways, Andria felt much more inner anguish around her daughter than her son. As she spoke to me during her last weeks, there was some sense of resigned peace around Alec - his life and his death. With Kate, however, I heard unspoken questions, shadows of guilt, unresolved pain. The few mentions made of Kate in earlier pages pretty much summed up the information Andria shared over the two years I knew her. In fact, I will admit to being surprised to hear that Kate died nearly 6 years AFTER Alec, and just a few years before I met Andria. And so, we are left with only these vague hints from a mother, and bitter words from a brother to remember a woman who also lived, breathed, and walked the earth. Katherine Williams: September 23, 1957 - March 13, 2006.

Andria

There was one incident during our time in Chicago, which did turn out to be significant for Alec. He had been very interested in Martial Arts for some time and had tried various teachers who didn't satisfy him. He had read widely on the subject and watched a number of videos. I once went into a store with him where he was looking for videos on Philippine Martial Arts and they turned out to have quite a number, all of which he wanted. I bought all $600 worth which made me very famous at that store. But from those variations on Martial Arts, he evolved his own form. Typically he wanted an independent form - not someone else's.

One evening, around 8 pm, Alec and I were sitting quietly in our place reading, when we heard a scream from outside. It was a woman, and I've never heard such terror in my life. Alec picked up a knife from his collection and said "call 911" and walked out into the alley behind the condo building, from which the scream had come. By the time he arrived, a car was just disappearing around the corner and there was nothing he could do. But I think he was pleased with himself that he had the guts to simply go out there to do anything he could, regardless of the danger involved. He also learned that he could handle police quite well. A patrol car arrived as he was standing there in the alley with a knife and asked him why he had it. He calmly explained that he had heard the scream and come out, and that they would have grabbed a weapon too under such circumstances. The police seemed to agree, letting him leave. The incident gave him a sense of his own courage, his own ability to act, and this was good for him.

Alec

re: Martial - Mantis wrist locks. Similar to knife fighters freeing-from-grab moves. Bear in mind Folsom and Kyusho about wrist locks - in mantis look for shortcuts, killshots are open - use them - instructor favors "paralyzed arm" (p4a)

Where ANYBODY has a possible weapon in their hands, get one in yours. In Combat, I don't need to contextualize, I just do it. Thus, Peace. (16c)

There is nothing more useless than a mis-timed Messiah. (14c)

Flai kicks used vs. round & Thai kicks if you move in - maybe in combo - inside flail to knee/thigh followed by outside to groin/haral solar plex - elbow & licking palm follow. Dervishing may be used for vertebral twist knockout/break. (14d)

Don't be afraid to do the impossible: what you don't know can't stop/harm you. (26d)

Hate and 3 Blessings (#14)

3 Kisses
From Satanas
Or from somewhere else
Strength
Brains
Brutality
Will have to see me through
Walk my night
Which lasts all through the day
Mirrors on my eyes
To reflect your imperfection
To hide the feral beast
And the hardness in my eyes
I brandish chains
I cherish scars
I love my brother blade
Not yet human
Nor yet beast
Perhaps, a part machine
I wait upon the wasting
The razing of your dream world

From where the blessings come

I know not

Satan?

You would wish it so

But Hate, I know whence that comes

My Hatred comes from you.

Reflection

One of the first and most constant challenges I had in sorting through Alec's journals was in separating out his notes around his online gaming life from his notes on his "real" life. Truthfully, the boundaries between "fact" and "fantasy" were not always significant to Alec in the same way that they might be to others, so every decision I have made as an editor is an imposition of my own understanding of reality onto Alec's thoughts as given shape through his words.

If I were to add up how much of my life is spent dealing in fact and how much is spent daydreaming, wondering, chasing thoughts around, worrying about things that never happen, fantasizing about the future, mulling over things I should have said, imagining myself in different scenarios, filling my mind with characters from a book, scenes from a movie, and so on - I would have to conclude that my life is most often lived in the world of fantasy, with only a minimal toehold in fact. Reality is a slippery concept at best, and in Alec's world, is perpetually fluid. I particularly enjoyed this random memory from Andria as a kind of intersection of realities in the ongoing creation of Alec.

Andria

Within a year of our moving back to Rochester, Alec would make only occasional outings to a bookstore or a shop run by a friend. But even that didn't last for long. Soon, he left the house only when he needed to see his doctor, or on occasion to visit the Psychologist he had been working with since he was 17. Alec had become interested in mysticism, and healing methods of various kinds - a field in which the psychologist was also interested. So, he would go, not to discuss his problems, but because he wanted to have a conversation on this subject with somebody competent and understanding. He would even book two appointments back-to-back so that they could have a good long time to talk. Once in a while, I would also see this man for questions on how to handle problems that arose with Alec, or my alcoholic daughter. The doctor seemed equally interested in Alec's works, and would encourage me to have Alec come back to see him.

Alec

Book order:
Llewellyn (on sale)* Meet Your Planet - KO17-6.418
100 Days to Better Health, Good Sex, and Long Life*
- K833-8.98
Temple Magic* - L274-3.98
Esoteric Rune Magic* - K174-6.00
Sensual Living* - K160-6.48
Seeds of Magic* - L865-4.98
A Grimoire of Shades: Witchcraft, Paganism and Magic
- K659-16.95
Northern Mysteries and Magic - KO47-19.98
Tortnos Serpene* - K743-6.48

A cohabitant consciousness/soul sibling - draw Clowes' attention to Tuatha De Danaan; a qualitative change in life - mab given newness - schiz fallout. (p2)

(Margin note) schizophrene: sufferer of schizophreneform or schizotyical disorder (p3)

The fits ending in unconsciousness of Delta level - they bear evidence of Samadhi, Investigate! Along with shaking, chi sweeps, body rushes, etc. - all have equivalents in the wisdom/mystic/magick traditions of being "god intoxicated." 6b

Through anti-psychotics, I have tasted your sanity - my response: DEATH FIRST! (6b)

A viable definition of schizophrenia would be the forcible acceptance by the subject (at whatever its cognitive and emotional level) of inherent quantum and nonlinear dynamic nature of the universe. Unless they dis chaos, it's no wonder they get bent. (10d)

Study fricke, juju, contomble, voodoo, etc., yergamine shot with blood on lips, barely nubile, shooting bck vs. organized bourgeois through dying is illustration. Study natural drugs in connection with above cults and witchcraft and McKenna as well as India book, and thuggeehashishim-assassination. (11b)

What do I ask? What do I say? I simply know it's time for action. But what action? Freestyle shamanism, bloody as painful, scarring dangerous as might be, perhaps the answer? (p8a)

Find me a woman as will nurse such a thing as I am, and she shall have a man who will go to the grave in her protection. I will convert and change in those ways

I can to make myself right to her (but will not provide child.) (13c)

<u>Two Girls</u> (#3)

Two girls
On the beach
Wearing Black
Turtlenecks, I think

I'll just sit and look sometimes,
Until they go away
They're beautiful
It's evening
Breeze is cool
Ocean's cold
Surf is quiet

Are they together?
They must be

Rian (#5)

Blue-grey lips and pale eyes
Softened angularity
A shadow cast
A moment held
A chemise
On the shoulder
Clinging,
Yet to fall entirely
I love you Rian
(Rian sound)
B+D+G riff 1x
B+D+G riff 2x w/vox
(guitar vol. swells riff)

Velvet Touch (#11)

Remove that velvet shirt
Standing at an angle
Your breasts may tumble free
And I would kiss them

Touch my tongue to yours
And drink from those fine red lips
Hold me in your velvet mouth
I will sing to you

Hands glide over softness
Cascading over warmth
One hand rests between
One hand continues flowing

Fingers that massage
Fingers find your mouth
Fingers that gain entry
Fingers taken in

Both hands are inside you
Continue their cascade.

Reflection

"Fits ending in unconsciousness... investigate!" I would like to think that my own response to "shaking, chi sweeps, body rushes" and "unconsciousness of Delta level" would be a driving curiosity. I would love to think that I would interpret these afflictions as a possible sign of being "god-intoxicated."

There has long been a debate around the recognition that when people who have been diagnosed with any form of mental health issue report hearing the voice of God, it is generally viewed as proof of their illness, whereas if a "normal" person makes that claim, it is seen as proof of their advanced state of enlightenment (at least among those who share their faith.) Once someone has been labeled as a "schizophrene," their perceptions of reality are safely sidelined under the cluster of associated symptoms, including the withdrawal from reality, illogical patterns of thinking, delusions, and hallucinations. The schizophrene is considered to be "disturbed." There is no doubt that Alec is "disturb-ing." And, clearly, he had trouble functioning within the parameters of "normal" society. But who am I to say that he is a victim of a debilitating mental/physical disease and NOT a god-intoxicated being with a mission to disturb the illusions of those around him into recognizing a greater truth. Perhaps, I am part of that ongoing mission. Who's to say?

Andria

Alec became unable to work in his studio. Again, he had a marvelously well-equipped set-up, but his physical strength began to wane from the illness he was born with. He could no longer move around heavy equipment, and besides from having a guitar at hand at all times, he didn't do any more serious work on his music. Instead, since he was reading so widely on so many subjects - psychology, mysticism, shamanism, and healing methods of the East, physics and astronomy theories for the universe - I bought books on a wide range of subjects for him. In fact, I probably gave him more books than he actually needed, but he knew I enjoyed finding things for him so he always accepted them very graciously. He was an extremely thoughtful person and because he knew I liked the feeling of having helped him, he would accept things he didn't really need.

Alec was attentive to me as well. He enjoyed my interest in jewelry and would give his opinion about particular pieces when I asked. He also encouraged me to visit a friend who was dying of cancer, even though it meant his being alone for a period of time - something that required enormous courage on his part. He often told me that I was his best friend.

For all this, as was his habit, he began to take bits and pieces to formulate a whole theory of his own, and he would come up and read pieces to me at night-time, when he thought he put something very well or had hit on a new concept. I distinctly remember an occasion when he brought together in one two-hour speech, quotations from several philosophers - Bertram Russell, Nietzsche (whom he liked very much), along with words from the beat generation poets, and lyrics from various musicians - Jimi Hendrix, John Coltrane, Miles Davis. He wove them all together into one coherent whole and it was marvelous to hear. I suggested he keep a journal of all these thoughts - that there was, in all probability, the making of a book in these notes and pieces he wrote at night. This he did do, and he worked at that until just a few months before his death.

Alec

Margin note: During Lyn trip, make sure I have legal representation. (2b)

Mom's Lyn visit: the truth of solitude has been made real to me. No shoulder, and worse, no possibility of one. The world has nothing for me but the fulfillment of my final CURSE. (5b)

Do at least one positive fuckin' thing: write Reeve and offer help - enclose Harner's Shaman book and remember Atavistic Nostalgia as key for healing of nerves (7b)

Today's alchemists are those in Quantum Mechanics and Chaology. (9b)

Past avatars (save Merlin?) have evolved from self to cosmic consciousness - I am moving from self to kaos consciousness. (9b)

My quantum consciousness is not in error, simply qualitatively different - not "meandering mind" or any such nonsense. (10b)

My system is no system, nor is it a theory; it is the phenomenation of question. (10b)

The Vedas list 6 kinds of master: I'm number 7 and cappin' it off. (10b)

Study natural drugs in connection with above cults and witchcraft and McKenna as well as India book, and thuggeehashishim - assassination. Self-healing, study - when using rusty pipe, sharpened wood (or anything where fingerprints may damage - find glove or cloth), find heavy cloth, towel, etc. Consider materials for maximum psychological effects. - (11b)

Terence, Rupert, Ralph, DMMT (Maybe Pete and Frater and Yuledove) but DMT, I felt it - here is salvation, Art, the book, Drs. Arnold and Gilberg perhaps can help - DMT is worth the risk, risk is a shaman's job, no more crying in the wilderness, remember you were born in a psychedelic state and remain in such. As to DMT - I'm not afraid. (1c)

Things will happen because I AM WHO I AM NOT (re: Old Test.) (re: 2001) (re: above notes on divinity and going beyond.) (14c)

Tarot reading today - day past blood (and burning) oath... Ultimately at this level (Draconic) the only problems presented are of your making. Family difficulties served as catalysts to bring me to this state. (19c)

Wait a minute; conversion of consciousness to tachyon form (perhaps quantum stuff, investigate) and possibly be present everywhere (in our universe, CMT paradigm), also fly, zip, what-have-you through wormholes (Gates) to alternate universe. Thusly, such finite universe idea, bound or unbound. Since quanta are postulated to be black holes (check CMT), white holes are about as well serving as 5-D conduits, this makes white holes possible, probably, needed. Thus Gates can, will exist, and following the above may well (hell, will!) provide access to the causal realm. Pure chaos. Wowie Zowie!!! (5d)

Ran into Krishnaji - heavy learning - the feeling he gave "of LOVE the same way I HATE," the fucker. Almost faked me out but I caught the learning he was cool enough NOT to teach. (17d)

I do not operate by discipline, but by selective obsessions. Freedom has no cornerstone, nor can it exist with one. I don't plod toward thing; I get them in my sights and sprint. All the above are lights to illuminate my own fundamental fucking stupidity. (38d)

WRITING PROJECTS (as noted by Alec throughout his journals)

Alchemy of Hate (14d)

Note: Start writing erotica. (16d)

The Book of Unbecoming
The Book of Living Death
The Book of Unapparent Cataclysm (25d)

Write book revising/reviewing astrology in light of quantum/fractal/chaos theory - check with P. Carroll for arguments/impressions/Preface. (28d)

"Death by Internet" - radioactivity transmitted via CRT screens w/added addictive (pleasurable?) properties resulting in compulsive use of leukemia causing information on net, massive computer virus kills humans via x-rays and encrypted radio-active (and microwave) Add addictive factor (brain opiate stimulus) Study systems! Encrypt lethal info so as to be released when exposed to appropriate stimuli - tech. KILLS ... Check Catastrophe theory and bio plague reports and S.T.P. transmission via radiation/query - can radioactivity act as carrier for addictive viral groups? (20d)

Winter Silence (her name): She has the Winter-blue eyes and Celtic weave tattoos, she all tawny-skinned, copper-haired; beauty, gentleness and strength, her essences. She is higher than language in form, communication, expression, and beyond the caprice of man and nature in formation. Her embrace is sweet drowning of all senses plus those past the five. She need not speak. Hers is the eloquence of silence, for the truth that is spoken is not truth, so is she true. She is illuminated, radiant - not with sunlight, but her own. Tall, some winter country. (23d)

Blonde Girl (#6)

Blonde girl with her tattoo
Speaking French or German...
I don't know either
Lives with a brunette
Who wears an eye patch and speaks Latin
I don't understand
Where do these people come from
Entropy sets in...
On night she's Lulu
Drawing stares and sighs
Decadence and kohl-rimmed eyes

Next night another sex?
Noel Coward's Lawrence
Her tuxedo will out-do mine

Then she's Kate (in the)
Taming of the Shrew
Am I Petruchio? I must be so.

Then it's Joan D'Arc
And I will be
Her Champion

She is every woman
More, every man, and yet
The more I know her
The more truth I see behind those eyes.

Reflection

The mind speeding up as the body slows down. A story that Andria related to me numerous times is of an occasion that took place in her kitchen. She was there, cooking, when Alec came in and sat down at the table, clearly wound up about something. He then launched into, as she remembered it, a two hour stream of consciousness monologue during which he filled the air with the names of philosophers, scientists, musicians, mathematicians, mystics, and others - simultaneously admiring and debating their thoughts, while weaving together and articulating alternative constructs out of his own grey matter. Andria admitted to me that she wasn't able to follow it all, but she was moved by the force of his thoughts, and the inner excitement he showed in exploring that mental landscape and discovering alternative trails and new vistas.

By every common standard, the story of Andria and Alec is a tragic one - a difficult tale of struggle, unfulfilled lives, and premature endings. But, it is also a window into the love between a mother and son, and the joy of friendship between two damaged souls who simply accept one another while sharing the journey that has been set before them. And what souls are not damaged in one way or another? And whose life is not tragic at some time along the way? And how beautiful is it to have been known and accepted and loved as we pass through?

Andria

He had an incredible amount of courage to endure the anxiety attacks he did without any sort of medication. While he was given Xanax in as great a dosage as they could prescribe, he needed it all together at one time, taken at night, to be able to eat and to have any hope of keeping the food down. This meant that he had to get through the rest of the time without medication. His days were often a stream of waking nightmares and panic attacks - similar to Post Traumatic Stress Disorder. As time went on, this became more and more difficult. It is a testament to his inner strength that he continued to work, read and write in spite of these hardships.

I clearly remember one nightmare he had. In this, he had been made executioner of the world. The roads were lined with crucifixes, and Alec was being forced to choose who would live and who would die. I had learned early on that I could not intervene in these episodes, but that it helped somehow for him to just talk his way through it.

Alec

Med logs (from April 1999?) – found in a spiral notebook.

April 4. Early morn - reg dose - eat sleep

April 4, 11:00 pm - reg dose eat + sleep

Aril 6, early morn - reg dose - eat sleep - relieve pain in gut + FREAKOUT + ½ dose + ½ dose

April 6 night reg dose + ½ eat sleep + relieve gut pain / 7th an ½ of reg dose same reasons

April 7 night: reg dose eat + sleep

April 8 night: reg dose - eat sleep - 4th 2:00 am extra amount dose - shakes

April 9th late night: reg dose - eat sleep - shaky

April 10th latenight: as above - 1 dose extra - shakes (speed style) - fuckin useless because of assholes

April 11 night: doses 2 SHAKES/freakouts

April 12 latenight: reg dose - eat sleep - speeding

April 13 night: dose - eat sleep - still speeding

April 14 night: ½ d e+s

April 15 night: ½ d e+s

April 16 night: ½ d e+s

April 18 night reg d. e+s shakes ½ d. blood shakes, puked

April 19 night: reg d. e+s - shakes - reg dose. - Lockdown.

April 20 late night reg d. - e+s - speeding (bleeding) d extra

April 21 night reg d - e+s - speed bleed 1 d. extra

April 22 late night reg d e+s / 25 identical to 21

April 23 late morning reg. d. e+s / 26 as 24 blood
April 24 late night reg. d. e+s

All formulas are flown, dealing with a heavy attack is never the same twice, it's down to improv and hope. (p4a)

Re: the above you will suffer, let none dissuade you - radical pain control for radical pain. Otherwise I just stave off the inevitable. No more loadedness, it gets in the way. (p7a)

Nidinksy: God is a fire in the head - most drugs put it out. I can't have that. Those that I use merely cause it to burn low for short time. But unchecked the fire will burn me up (fits, spasms, starvation, etc.) I must keep it alive, strong but sometimes banked, lest I die or go mad. In quantum terms, I am a receiver being constantly hit with info and responding to it physically. (5b)

Problem: premature decrepitude/doomed alienation. (p8a)

Christianity = church of the stolen corpse and the necro-fucking of it. (1b)

Any absolute that humanity projects is already and naturally insufficient to meet the demands needed to fulfill the concept. (21b)

Holding visceral knowledge and powers is like being stapled by the hands to a 2x4. The skeptics wipe up the blood and call it catsup; the believers spray catsup of their own upon the wounds and call it "divine blood" or some such crap, while the fakes spray themselves with catsup and howl for attention. The fakes count money with uninjured hands, the skeptics laugh at the requests for medical aid and believers weep with joy anytime you scream. FUCK 'EM ALL! KILL! (1c)

I expect my last curse will be cast at my death. Pay attention to my last curse, it may be what I just said. (6b)

Going up to see mom about wide-awake nightmares generally don't work: banish yourself or crash except MAJOR emergencies. (14b)

Mom: has used MY abuse of her sleep as a threat to her longevity, thus to my last bastion of security i.e.: Fuck off or be helpless. There can be no love here between us - consider this under circumstance and my errors - but I did hear threat. (6c)

I do not seek my Mother for comfort at night out of (I hope) kindness but primarily I know too well what I am and what I am causes wakefulness and pain. The Ipssissumus process. (8c)

"Sanity" means permanent denial, while chronic schizo behavior means you see constantly but cannot live/accept/survive with it, thus dementia praecox, world catastrophe, etc. I must be wyrd 'cause I live with it, thrive on CHAOS; my definition of lost is: I know where I am HERE, everything else is out of places, same with time, it's all NOW, memory and prediction - crap. (7d)

The flashbacks and wide-awake nightmares are resonance from harmonics. Thus: cancel harmonics - cancel suffering. (38d)

There is no stop-start, only action at varying rates of vibration - harmonic... (37d)

Moving towards full kaos realization. Symptoms:
1) ideational, emotional and lingual are all stretching more chaos.

To communicate, I must pose/mask (and do not place interpretations on what is said!) or else am honest and make 5-10% of what I wish to express clear, at most (but I am interested in interpretations.)
2) senses (normal 5) have reached a new pitch - the blindingly fast seems slow, volume differentiation is hard between "reasonable norm" and going out of my head (Point 1: important - I can never fully remember what the pose/mask SAID) (Point 2: similarity in gnosis in precision of remembrance, but also flat out honesty.)

I am dependent for translation and transaction that humans speak or do, and while thus at the moment "Katedom" kills me, without you, Mom, I substitute another peddler of humanity. I cannot leave though I would to ease you, but for a potential assassin. (10c)

Tainted blood Tainted brain (#7)

No expert can explain

Diagnosis

Just a lie

None know such as I

Therapy

Needles

Scorn of all I meet

Drugs

Poisons

Sympathy no substitute for compassion

Insane

Schizoid

Paranoid psychotic

Rape by healers

Toy of doctors

Pet of arrogance

No part of your world

Except to provide stimulation

With the fractions of self that function

Gifted

Genius

Genocide my dream

Treat me as you will

I'm not dead

For all your help

I'll take you with me

I am why religion was created

Force of nature

Unstopped by well meant wounds

Not dead yet

Not dead yet

No goddammit,

I'm not dead yet.

Reflection

Perhaps more than any other, this section breaches the remaining distance between story and truth, character and self. Alec's medication diary is written in the same determined print as the rest of his journals - small, sometimes shaky, but legible. The nature of its detail forces it out of some poignant past, into a physically tangible present. Alec's thoughts abide within, and emerge from, a fragile, tremorous body - a body that seeks and rejects food, that longs for and suffers from sleep/lessness, one that craves medical relief while actively holding it at arms' length lest it change his sense of self. There is a raw self-awareness here that is disillusioning in the most concrete meaning of the term. Though others around him might understandably believe that Alec was delusional, Alec claimed himself in total, and fought for his own right to define his reality.

How often do we believe, as Andria did, that we are doing the very best we can within a given set of circumstances, to be present, compassionate, supportive - only to have our best efforts dismissed by the focus of our attentions as inadequate, or even harmful? Knowing Andria as I did, there is something acutely heartbreaking to me in knowing that she saw her willingness to remain with Alec during his waking nightmares as one of the finer moments of her parenting past, while Alec remembers only this moment where Andria "fails" him. Of course, I say "only" when the truth is that it is the only memory he committed to this journal. I choose to believe that he was driven to write about it because this episode stood out from the norm and brought these thoughts to the surface. As a sometime-journaler myself, I confess that I am most driven to pick up my pen when some experience jars me from the stream of the expected, and forces me to wrestle with a shift in my understanding of reality. Though it can sometimes be a joyful "high," it is more often a painful "low." The highs fit into my self-story - they are deserved, anticipated, and welcomed. The lows, on the other hand, are inevitably undeserved, and unappreciated. The journal receives my bitterness, self-pity, anger, or confusion - never talking back or challenging my perspective.

Andria

Alec knew he was going to die. He could feel it as his body functions were showing it. He never complained about it. It was a matter of pride that he should not complain. He would simply tell me that it was a bad day and ask for a quiet household, which he got. I postponed improvements to the house, necessary work around the property. I didn't have guests visit or stay. I kept it as quiet as possible so that he could sleep without interruption during the day and work without interruption at night.

I took a great deal of flack for this from a number of people who were convinced that I was pampering him. But the psychiatrist who prescribed for him said that this was the appropriate treatment for Alec in his condition and encouraged me to continue, handling as I had been doing. It was always amazing to me that the do-gooders and the people who knew better than I would go on telling me what I should be doing differently, even after I said he had a medical doctor, a psychiatrist, and a psychologist, all of whom said I was doing the right things, they still went on, insisting that I do things differently. I got very shut up with these people. Fortunately, I didn't tell Alec about all of this. He would have just demurred his feelings about that.

Alec

re: Clowes - all formulas are flown, dealing with a
heavy attack is never the same twice, it's down to
improv and hope. Also my relatives are retarded Nazi's
selling shit about me and mom. (p4a)

Fuck honor. If fulfilled, it's blamed. If not, you're
pissed on, including not living up to scum expectations.
(p9a)

Illuminating thought: enlightenment may be becoming
ONE by becoming MANY; observing the perpetual rising
and dissolution of personalities, each partaking of
perception upon different planes, without being or
overwhelming. Perception itself, observing its perceptions
with wonder. Every tick of a clock becomes worthy of
wonder when a new self is perceiving it with new senses
for the first and quite possibly last, time (never in the
phenomenal rate at which the clock, ticks and all,
changes, plus the flux betwixt you both and Universal
Chaos in general.) (24d)

Winter Candles (#8)

Candles of winter
Bode ill at dusk

Midnight howls so close
Frozen steps in twilight ice
Found each coming dawn
One step nearer every day
I count them as I pass
9, 10, 11, 12
And 13 never comes
I pray blood will fall upon the snow
When the 13th step has fallen
Will it be mine, will it be hers?
Will it be someone else's?
Death still stands at midnight
With blade poised yet to fall
And 13 I pray never comes
The beast will reach inside
The blade will fall
Death will come
I know not in what guise
But frozen steps I know
Steps I recognize
Winter candles keep them at bay
For please
Those steps are mine.

Reflection

When I think of Andria and Alec, this is how I picture them - two souls alone in their understanding of each other, protective of each other, beloved strangers to each other - finding solace in silence, even as that silence is filled with prose, poetry, and the awareness of time. I imagine a playwright giving words to the two actors on the stage, the set design at once comforting and claustrophobic. I hear them voicing their fears and making their peace in side-by-side soliloquies. Profoundly close in ways that mother and son rarely are, but held apart by design. The clock ticks into the silence as the two pass, shifting into the next scene.

Andria

So matters went, living very quietly together, sharing a few hours of the day before going to bed and he started to work. He was a great companion, and we had an extremely pleasant life together. Before it became too much for him, Alec loved to be hugged - often asking for them. Then, slowly but surely, he began to want to be alone, even from me. At times, our paths would only cross briefly in the morning, passing on the stairs. Now he would sometimes say, "I feel very small," meaning that I needed to be especially quiet.

So many things became a strain for him. We had been in the habit of watching videos, very special ones that we had taped for ourselves or had ordered. Alec began to struggle to do even that. I could see the tension in his body and his hands and could tell that he wasn't getting any real pleasure from it, except that we were sharing time. When the video was over, I told him that I appreciated seeing it, but thought it had been a demand on him, and that he shouldn't feel required to make these efforts. It was taking too much strength from him. I suggested we put off this particular ritual until he felt strong enough to do so again.

By now, I knew that it was likely that he would not ever feel stronger again, but it seemed kinder to work on the theory that he would be better some day. He needed to believe that someday he would return to the studio. He needed to believe that someday he would play and compose again. I wanted to bolster that belief in any way I could to give him comfort. And so, I continued to buy new equipment for his studio. I even bought a couple more guitars, which he liked immensely and demonstrated for me, but that was the only time he played them. He simply didn't have the strength any longer. He had the ideas and the skills - his "chops" as musicians would call them were very well held - but it was just too much of an effort for him to play.

In the spring of 1999, when his strength had gone to the point where he felt he could no longer work on music or on his book, he began to ask me for just really good mysteries to read which I was able to find for him. He had essentially been living downstairs - sleeping on the sofa (which had been bought for him when he was just two), and never venturing up to his own bedroom except to find a magazine or some such. (His room had been wall-to-wall magazines, including Playboy.) His cat, Zappa, stayed close to him, sleeping with him on the couch.

But the time came when he left Zappa on his own, and moved upstairs to his room - the only air-conditioned room in the house. I still made food for him and left it out so that he could eat at night, whenever he felt like it. But it was clear that his system was no longer handling food properly, and he began to eat very, very little. When he saw me, periodically, he would tell me that he wasn't going to have a very long life, and I would tell him that I understood and would miss him very much.

Alec

Chang Tzu - Don't draw life from death - not vampirism or Irish gloom. Don't look upon life as death's mirror image, absolutes replacing one another, but fractal continuum. The music of life is not the score of death, nor vice versa. (12b)

Turned 30 in 1999 - I experienced the trauma of re-birth in enlightenment and awareness, from Death in Da'ath. (24b)

Given Rupert's ideas of morphogenetic fields, is it enough that I (apparently) exist and by so doing set up a morphic resonance which will encourage humanity to evolve along similar (i.e. digging chaos) lines? Investigate. (10d)

I am a mask speaking, the mask of HGA. When the HGA needs no mask, I will be enlightened. (28d)

Girder Lusting (#18)

Girder lusting
Lacework in a field of night
Starless
Upon which I stand
Hand upon your long forgotten self
Flaking away at my fingers' touch
Like dried blood from a wound ill-closed
How long abandoned you have been
Among your steel brethren
That in your loneliness
You weep your rust around me
Like a veil

Reflection

Tucked into the books Alec left behind were tiny slips of paper, marking favorite passages, or puzzling concepts to be further investigated. Many of these markers were, in fact, scraps on which Andria had written notes to him - messages that he presumably read before tucking into whatever volume he was reading. Below is a sampling of these mother-to-son memos:

(There was a hole in the center of this note...) -
"She has had a 'hopeful' discussion with her boss.
Conversationally speaking, she left me stunned.
What's the appropriate response when
somebody discusses ... intellect ... Without
wanting to be a "meow" type person, I don't
think she has ever met a 'great intellect.'
Oswego State and ? don't attract such.

Eyedrops will ... a little late ... but expect
I'll go up around 9:30. Trust you will sleep a
lot.

*****

10:30 to hospital. From there, straight to Sue and
massage. Back about 2:00 - long enough to gulp
water. 2:30 Dr. Hanson. After that - kittens.
If I wander or revisit hospital, which I don't
expect to do, will message? more. Sorry it was
a bad night.

*****

10:00 - a college student named Phillipe (French pronunciation) is here working on the lawn in front. Intelligent, listens. When I go shopping, I'll tell him. He's capable of relaying a message to Rum (?) I trust that will prevent thunderous knocks on any door. I try! Love again, Mom

*****

According to Frank, by the way, Prozac is chemically very close to LSD. Interesting considering the reaction you had to it. Hope the night goes well for you - Love, Mom.

*****

Given the kind of day it's been, I couldn't guess what, if anything, you'd want to eat. I have sliced the beef roast - it's quite a good one - and there's a new kind of bread, supposed to be very good. Lots of green peppers in left veg bin, and you know where the carrots are. I may even stop being lazy and put one out for you. Course, just use the freezer if that's more likely. I added to the supply today and anytime you feel like a pizza, just let me know.

I do appreciate the information for Betsy, and the patient support you give me, when I dither about my dithering as to what's amiss with me. As a Mom, I do give you lots of chances to be helpful! Love you - Mom

Andria

One Saturday morning, he came downstairs for a very brief conversation and then went upstairs and I didn't see him again that day. He was suffering from a severe case of heartburn. I was concerned that it could be a heart attack, and suggested we go to the emergency room. He declined, and knowing that the stress of an emergency room on a Saturday night would be more than he could bear, I did not press the point. I made one last offer of bouillon to which he said, "Please Mom..." I took my cue, and headed to bed.

All night long, I heard him moving around, back and forth to the bathroom, clearly uncomfortable. The next day, I went up to leave a note for him, just letting him know my plans. He came out of the bathroom, looked at me and put a hand up, palm facing me, and simply backed away quietly, down the hall, into the studio. I remember thinking that he looked like a stranger to me in that moment - older, unrecognizable. I followed him down the hallway at a discrete pace, and then he just gently and silently closed the door in my face. That was the last time I saw him alive.

Later that day, I came up again to leave another note, and stumbled over his body. He was lying on the bathroom floor - his face relaxed and looking very young, his right hand clenched slightly. In his death, he looked much like he had looked when he was just two years old, taking a short nap.

I suspect that his heart had just given out. In England this is known as a "quick death" and I was grateful for it.

He had died quickly, and he had been serenely contemplating it, accepting it without any problem at all. He had his own theory of what happened after death, and he welcomed it. I did not like losing my son at 30, but it was good to know that he had been so secure about his future, and so convinced that it was going to be a better life for him.

Alec

The boy born doomed - his virility is poison (end)
And so he sits, a-planning still, buried in his barrow,
plans of stillborn nightmare; unending without waking,
plans of hate, til giving takes the place
of ruthless taking,
plans to send the world asunder, '
til something better rises,
a people who would not deny, his place beside their fire.
Cataclysm, Dearios, he strives to make come real,
so from human compost, will rise those whom he cannot
hate, for they give to him no cause,
and then his task completed then,
may he lie him down to die.
He will never know the beauty that his hate creates,
nor will he know the love of those who he had to slay.
He belongs to neither; pitied by the followers,
rejected by their past;
the love he bore was turned to acid, alchemy of state.

But he did play his part well, knowing he could not
wallow, unable to take his life;

and so he clung to hatred & made of her a wife and
their spawn was chaos,

the ravens and the grave,

and from such spawn were other born,

of peace he could not attain.

Hark well, listeners, hear me, the Doomed Boy is not still.
His shadow on your doorstep,

he strives against you yet.

For until you are past and gone,

and new ones see the sky,

he writhes in pain while cursing you

and with dead fingers searches for the final life,

your debt. (21d-22d)

Hawkings string theory universe theory proves the
limitation of senses available to consciousness in this
dimension, as does Kosko's Fuzzy Thinking -
consciousness ranges far further than the body can go.
We can probe Mars in Malkuth (to speak
Quabballistically), but we cannot escape the limitations
of Malkuth by using its tools. To reach Kether and
beyond, we must free consciousness from the chains
imposed by Malkuth and Malkuth thinkers, only then when

our sole tool not bound by Malkuth and its seeming laws may we escape to wherever else though the bodies designed for Malkuth remain in Malkuth, but they were not designed for the stars anyway. (5a)

Ya don't have to go FTL, ya just Go! Send quantum/fractal awareness; leave the body bit of oneself behind. (32d)   *FTL - Faster than Light

We ARE light, just moving slowly. The sunlight we ingest could be sapient life moving faster. WE could be ingested by other light. (29d)

Light = speed = freedom. Body of light is pure awareness. (27d)

Liquid Light (#16)

When brightness falls, from the sky
The liquid light
And butterflies
Will come
To taste the brilliance in the air
While you and I
Will glory upon the god-void frost
That the stars gave us a gift
And swim in rainbows

While in the air
Make love in every color
Make love in body mind and spirit
Peace has come at last

When brightness falls from the sky
The liquid light
And flowing shadows
Come to us
And share the taste of radiance
While you and I
Create a night
Arced with stars
And midnight rainbows
Swimming between prismatic lattice
The substance of the Bifrost

*Editor's note – In Norse mythology, **Bifröst** or **Bilröst**
is a burning rainbow bridge that reaches between
Midgard (the world) and Asgard, the realm of the gods.

Tigers (#10)

Tigers shoot straight to the sky
Don't know how, don't ask why
Just accept they just do it.

drum opening

4 count on hi hat

riff

riff with vox

solo

cut off

Riff – riff with vox – solo – cut off.

Postscript

I have, for the past year, been involved in an arduous effort - the results of which, very few, if any, will ever see. Though it is a contracted project - a specific writing assignment - it has been much, much more than a job. I have wrestled with this task in a way that I have never really struggled before, and even as it draws to a close, I continue to feel a bit like Jacob grappling with the angel through that long night of the soul.

My task emerged from the dying wish of a mother as she lay in her hospice room. Her son had predeceased her by over ten years - he, himself, having died at the young age of 30 after a lifetime of physical and mental illness resulting from a defective nervous system. During those years, however, he had also shown a brilliant, if sometimes brutal mind, along with a genuine gift for composing and playing the guitar. His mother had convinced him to keep a journal for the last few years of his life, and it was her strong desire that those journals be edited and published, so that others might somehow benefit from them.

Because she had come to trust me, and to respect my communication skills, and because she believed I would not judge her son, but recognize his gifts as she did, she asked me to take on this project. I agreed, and signed a contract that would be overseen by her attorney in charge of the trust fund she had created for this purpose. My friend, Andria, died a week later, leaving me with her son, Alec's, journals.

Immediately upon opening to the first page, I could see that this was going to be an enormous task. Alec's mind raced as did his nervous system - jumping quickly and without warning from a thought about physics, to a note about a karate move he wanted to study, to a line from a song, to a mystical revelation, to a list of medications, to a beatnik philosopher whose works he both admired and debated. Jumping into the pages of his journals required a certain steely resolve and a kind of focused breathing in order to stay engaged long enough to begin to see the connections and themes.

And, all the time I was immersing myself in Alec's world, I was fighting the knowledge that there was no one left on this planet who really knew or cared about this young man. His whole family was gone, and, having been a paranoid recluse, very few others knew him at all. Who would want to read the thoughts of an angry, sometimes violent young man whose life seemed to mean so very little even when he was alive? He burned there in the confined rooms of his house for a few short years, and then burned out. His mother had loved him, but she too was gone.

A peculiar thing has happened, though, over these past 12 months. I have come to love Alec. I love his courage in engaging so fully with the tiny bit of this earth that he occupied. I love his curiosity about anything and everything - along with his passionate (and well-informed) opinions. I love his attachment to his mother and his cat, Zappa. I love his poetry, which takes me by surprise every time it appears on a page - and moves me. I love his self-deprecating humor. I love his persistent search for meaning to his life, and his belief that his meaning would become realized upon his death.

I will continue to struggle with this writing project until the day it is finally released. But I have been blessed by it as well. It has taught me something about faith - that sometimes one has to look long and hard to discover God's grace - but that love is always, ALWAYS there. It has taught me that we sometimes have to dig deep and stay attentive and believe that there is someone inside of that crazy/annoying/scary/confusing/off-putting person in front of us who is worthy of a mother's love, and created out of God's love. And once we discover that person, our own lives are enriched beyond measure.

You won't read this book. It is quite possible that nobody will ever read this book. But, I am grateful to have read God's heart in the journals of a young man who was once loved by his mother - and who is now loved by me as well.

Appendix A –
Books from Alec's collection, saved by Andria

Carroll, Peter J. *Liber Kaos*. York Beach: Samuel Weiser, 1992

Fortune, Dion. *Psychic Self-Defense*. York Beach: Samuel Weiser, 1993

Fry, Christopher. *The Lady's not for Burning*. London: Oxford University Press, 1950

Fukami, Seizan. *Exorcism: Gateway to a New Life*. Tokyo: Tachibana Shuppan, 1992

Godwin, David. *Godwin's Cabalistic Encyclopedia, 3rd Edition*. St. Paul: Llewellyn, 1994

Gray, William. *Inner Traditions of Magic*. New York: Samuel Weiser, 1970

McKenna, Terence. *Food of the Gods*. New York: Bantam Books, 1992

Plotkin, Mark J. *Tales of a Shaman's Apprentice*. New York: Viking Penguin, 1993

Spare, Austin Osman. *Two Tracts on Cartomancy*. London: Fulger, 1997

Stewart, R.J. *Merlin: The Prophetic Vision and The Mystic Life*. London: Arkana, 1986

Symonds, John, and Kenneth Grant, eds. *The Magical Record of the Beast 666: The Diaries of Aleister Crowley*. London: Gerald Duckworth & Co., 1983

Vitebsky, Piers. *The Shaman*. London: MacMillan, 1995

Wilson, Colin. *The Occult*. New York: Random House, 1971